{ BALANCED }
RAW

{ BALANCED }

RAW

COMBINE RAW AND COOKED FOODS for Optimal Health, Weight Loss, and Vitality

TINA LEIGH, C.H.H.C., C.P.C.

Founder of Haute Health, www.HauteHealthNow.com

FAIR WINDS
PRESS
BEVERLY, MASSACHUSETTS

© 2013 Fair Winds Press
Text © 2013 Tina Leigh
Photography © 2013 Fair Winds Press

First published in the USA in 2013 by
Fair Winds Press, a member of
Quayside Publishing Group
100 Cummings Center
Suite 406-L
Beverly, MA 01915-6101
www.fairwindspress.com

17 16 15 14 13   1 2 3 4 5

ISBN: 978-1-59233-551-0

Digital edition published in 2013
eISBN: 978-1-61058-741-9

Library of Congress Cataloging-in-Publication Data available

Cover and book design by Carol Holtz
Book layout by Duckie Designs
Photography by Glenn Scott Photography
Food styling by Jessica Weatherhead

Printed and bound in China

The information in this book is for educational purposes only. It is not intended to replace the advice of a physician or medical practitioner. Please see your health care provider before beginning any new health program.

I dedicate this book to . . .

My mom, for ensuring we had vegetables at lunch and salad with our evening meal

My family and friends, for believing no dream of mine is ever out of reach

The many leaders, teachers, and healers who have guided me through my health journey and helped me develop an appreciation for holistic self-care

And my clients, who continually share their unique gifts, personalities, goals, and needs, and motivate me to grow in my knowledge of health and nutrition

{ Contents }

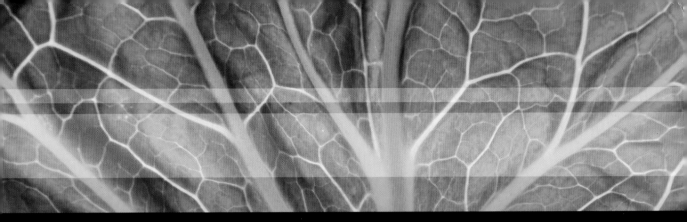

PART 2: THE BALANCED RAW SYSTEM 46

{ Part 1 }

ADOPTING THE
BALANCED RAW
LIFESTYLE

CHAPTER 1

WHY BALANCED RAW IS A NUTRITIONAL ALL-STAR

IMAGINE A DIET FREE OF ANY FOOD THAT IS PROCESSED OR ARTIFICIAL. A diet in which canned or cooked foods are considered void of nutrients. A diet in which bottled condiments like salad dressings, marinades, and concentrated oils made from soybeans, peanuts, and corn are excluded. This diet is rich in raw and organic vegetables, fruits, seaweeds, nuts, sprouted grains, seeds, and legumes. In most cases, animal products are omitted, but some followers choose to supplement their heavy roughage intake with raw beef, dairy, and fish.

This diet is known as "raw" because it includes only those foods that are unaltered, made from scratch, and eaten in their most natural form. Although some raw foodists eat a small portion of cooked foods, to preserve the nutritional content most fare is eaten cold, at room temperature, or warmed to heats never exceeding 118°F (48°C).

MANY HAVE ADOPTED THE DIET IN THE NAME OF HEALTH. ADVOCATES, CALLED "RAW FOODISTS," believe eating mostly uncooked and unprocessed foods is the gateway to a disease-free existence and by doing so they thrive from eating a Living Foods Diet, a name interchangeable with "Raw." To some, and even you, this diet may sound perfect. But is it?

A new raw food approach, or as I like to call it, "Balanced Raw," is gaining momentum and being recognized as the program of choice for optimum health, sustainability, and balanced nutrition because it includes a variety of both raw and cooked foods that are low in fat and rich in enzymes, macronutrients, vitamins, and minerals. Even some of the most respected and steadfast raw foodists are converting to this new approach, and their swing from "high raw" (75 percent raw or more) to "balanced raw" (50 percent or more) is due to the belief that cooked foods are nourishing and grounding and that cooking enhances the absorption of nutrients in certain foods, as is the case with tomatoes. A balanced raw diet is lower in fat than a 100 percent raw diet because it is not heavily reliant on high-fat nuts for protein, and instead includes cooked legumes and grains. This is essential as low-fat diets help to protect against high cholesterol, heart disease, diabetes, stroke, and even cancer.

Furthermore, a balanced diet of raw and cooked foods is common in Asian cultures, which include some of the healthiest and longest-living people on the planet. And in a 2012 article in *The Huffington Post*, author Isaac Eliaz, M.D., M.S., L.Ac., suggests that eating cooked foods brings warmth to the gut and increases digestive fire, resulting in more efficient digestion and assimilation— something you will come to understand is essential for optimum health.

In a January 2012 interview in *Veg News*, Victoria Boutenko, a pioneer of the green smoothie movement and follower of a 100 percent raw diet for more than a decade, shared her conversion to a part-time raw approach. She said, "What is more nourishing: steamed asparagus or cashew nuts? Lightly cooked red cabbage or an ounce of raw almond butter? A baked apple or a slice of a raw dessert? I know now these cooked foods are nutritionally superior, but I didn't know then to ask these questions." Victoria affirms that by eating some cooked foods we are exposed to variety, and that eating cooked vegetables is better for our health than eating a cup of nut butter.

Chad Sarno, a revered chef who for years developed raw menus for restaurants around the globe, has also recently changed his rawtarian tune. After getting a complete blood panel, he found his cholesterol and triglyceride levels to be deep in the unhealthy range. He attributed the disappointing results to eating a traditional raw foods diet. He believed for many years that an abundance of nuts provided a healthy source of fat and protein. However, after receiving the results of his blood work, he realized the negative health consequences of eating these foods in excess. He immediately put himself on a part-time raw diet consisting of mostly vegetables (raw and cooked), cooked grains, and legumes, and was astonished when after only four months his cholesterol dropped one hundred points and his triglyceride levels came back into the healthy range.

This book isn't just for people who eat only raw foods and want to enhance their diet with cooked foods. If you have been eating a diet composed mainly of cooked foods and want to convert to a greater percentage of raw, you will also be enlightened because this book is all about balance. Whether shifting from high raw to balanced raw, or the opposite, the goal is to help you find middle ground. The program and recipes will be your guides to health transformation and will support you no matter what your eating habits are today. Through these pages you will be introduced to lifestyle tools, resources, and meals that will bring equilibrium to your scales.

WHY THE EMERGENCE OF BALANCED RAW?

The raw food diet began more than a century ago, and in the late 1970s the persuasive movement erupted, based on the belief that cooking denatures or destroys essential enzymes in our food, and that eating living enzymes is the secret to longevity and sustained health. The raw diet generally consists of unprocessed, ideally organic, and entirely uncooked or dehydrated fruits and vegetables, some sprouted grains and beans, and a hefty dose of nuts and seeds. A large percentage of raw foodists also adhere to a vegan diet, one without animal foods of any kind. There is a significantly smaller population of raw followers who choose to consume raw dairy, meat, and fish.

One-hundred-percent raw foodists miss out on the health benefits provided by eating certain foods cooked, such as sweet potatoes, carrots, and tomatoes, which deliver more nutritive value when eaten lightly cooked than raw, and are easier to digest. This is an important factor because the value of a food being easily digestible is essential for optimum health, which I will explain further in a moment.

Many health experts, such as Joel Fuhrman, M.D., author of *Eat to Live*, suggest that having a large percentage of your diet rich in raw foods holds tremendous nutritive power because of the delivery of active food enzymes, antioxidants, and minerals. Studies also indicate lightly cooked, sprouted, and fermented foods, a balance of macronutrients, minimal consumption of oil, and the elimination of preservatives, additives, and processed foods, are even more essential to achieving weight loss, vitality, and optimum health.

"Certainly, there are benefits to consuming plenty of raw fruits and vegetables," says Fuhrman. "These foods supply us with high nutrient levels and are generally low in calories, too. Eating lots of raw foods is a key feature of an anti-cancer diet style and a long life. . . . But are there advantages to eating a diet of all raw foods and excluding all cooked foods? The answer is a resounding 'no.' In fact, eating an exclusively raw food diet is a disadvantage. Excluding all steamed vegetables and vegetable soups from your diet narrows your nutrient diversity and has a tendency to reduce the percentage of calories from vegetables in favor of nuts and fruits, which are lower in nutrients per calorie."

You have probably heard others say, or may have even said yourself, "I eat 80, 90, or even 100 percent raw." For years, this has been a simple way to affirm one's dedication to the raw food movement. Balanced Raw, however, is defined by the integration of many key principles, and not just about eating raw, so after embracing this lifestyle, you may simply say, "I am balanced."

The Balanced Raw approach brings calm and order to the somewhat confusing and conflicting world of nutrition because it explains all the reasons why balance is essential and urges you to find value in consuming both raw and cooked foods in addition to understanding the value of low-fat and unprocessed foods.

REDUCE FAT CONSUMPTION FOR INCREASED SATIETY

As said previously, the genuine efforts made by raw foodists to eat in the name of good health have, in some cases, had the opposite effect. For example, followers of the traditional, high-fat raw food diet eat raw desserts and snacks to maintain adequate caloric intake, and rely on hight-fat ingredients to actualize richness, density, and texture. Desserts such as puddings, ice cream, and tarts are often made with cashew or macadamia nut fillings, and the blending of soaked almonds or pecans with nut butters or oil is a technique used to create dessert crusts. Other acceptable sources of calories and richness in the traditional raw food diet are nut pâtés, raw cheeses, and nut-based sauces and spreads.

However, eating a high-fat diet does not necessarily help you feel sated. Satiety, the feeling of fullness that signals you have had enough to eat, is achieved by hormonal and neurological messages sent to your brain from your gut. The volume of the foods in your meal contributes to a feeling of satiety. The neurological message is signaled via nerve receptors in your stomach that tell your brain your gut is stretching to capacity and you can stop eating. The second message is sent when a digestive hormone known as cholecystokinin is released. When you eat a voluminous meal, more of this hormone is excreted, ensuring your brain knows it has had enough, whereas less is produced when you eat a smaller meal or snack.

John McDougall, M.D., in the profound movie *Forks over Knives*, uses the example that when you eat about 500 calories of complex carbohydrates such as grains and vegetables, your stomach fills to capacity, the signal of satiety is sent, and you feel full. In the case of 500 calories of protein, the weight and volume comparison is significantly less than 500 calories of grains or vegetables, your stomach is filled to less capacity, and you must eat more to activate the receptors. Fats leave you the most dissatisfied because when you consume 500 calories of concentrated fats such as oil and even nuts, the weight and volume are so insignificant that your receptors are left untriggered, causing you to overeat to feel sated. This is why you can have a bag of almonds at your desk, munch on them by the handful, and almost never feel satisfied.

MAINTAIN A HEALTHY ESSENTIAL FATTY ACID RATIO TO PREVENT AND REDUCE INFLAMMATION

In addition to monitoring the quantity of fats in your diet, understanding the quality and ratio of certain types of fats, particularly essential fatty acids (EFAs), is key in either promoting or decreasing the negative effect fats can have on your health.

Essential fatty acids are coined as such because our bodies can't manufacture them, so to realize their essential health benefits, you must get them from food sources. There are three distinct groups, with the two most critical being omega-3 and omega-6 fatty acids. For optimum health, you need an appropriate balance of the two. According to Joseph Mercola, M.D., a doctor of osteopathy and expert in holistic health and nutrition healing, a healthy ratio of omega-6s to omega-3s is 1:1, yet shockingly, the ratio of the standard American diet falls at an average of 30:1!

Omega-3 fats are highly concentrated in flax, chia, and hemp seeds, spinach, arugula, walnuts, sea vegetables such as chlorella and spirulina, and romaine lettuce, while omega-6 fatty acids are abundant in most nuts, especially almonds, sesame and sunflower seeds, and corn, safflower, sunflower, peanut, and soybean oils. Today, omega-6 fatty acids are also found in animal products because of the large quantity of omega-6-containing grains they are fed.

Omega-3 fatty acids are the supergood guys, and even though we need omega-6 fatty acids, the amount required for optimal health is nowhere near the amount many people consume today.

WHY DO YOU WANT MORE OMEGA-3S?

A diet too high in omega-6 fatty acids and lacking in omega-3s wreaks havoc on your system. The molecular structure of omega-3 fatty acids has blood-thinning properties, which allows them to circulate through the body efficiently, according to the University of Maryland Medical Center. The center's studies affirm omega-3 compounds protect against inflammatory illnesses such as heart disease and diabetes by contributing to lower LDL cholesterol, triglyceride, and blood pressure levels, and they reduce risk of Alzheimer's and stroke by preventing hardening of the arteries and slowing plaque development.

In her book, *Raw & Beyond: How Omega-3 Nutrition Is Transforming the Raw Food Paradigm*, Victoria Boutenko explains that having omega-6s in the diet is just as essential as having omega-3s, but that too much promotes inflammatory disease. This is because omega-6 fatty acids compete for the same enzymes necessary to convert the EFAs from a saturated form into one that can be utilized and absorbed by the body. According to Mehmet Oz, M.D., because of its molecular structure, omega-6s win in this competition if the ratio of omega-6s to omega-3s is greater than 1:1.

I understand this is not joyful news if you have been following a high-fat, raw food diet, but the good news is the risk of these conditions can be reduced or even reversed with an increase of omega-3s.

You may now be wondering how to achieve a healthy balance of these essential fatty acids. The answer is simple. Rather than worrying about a precise ratio, work toward replacing omega-6-containing oils with ground flax, chia, and hemp seeds. In addition, reducing your intake of fats and oils to 10 percent or less of your total calories will help keep you from consuming too many omega-6s. For example, if you aim to consume 2,000 calories per day, the total calories from fats you will want to consume is 200, or no more than approximately 2 tablespoons of nuts, seeds, avocado, nut butter, or oil.

A word of caution: Although they are highly nutritious, omega-3s are very unstable, meaning they go rancid quickly and should never be heated. This is why flax and hemp seed oils are always found in the refrigerated section of your market. They begin to denature (or become rancid) at room temperature. Ingesting rancid oils promotes the formation of free radicals and with free radicals comes an increase of disease. You will learn more about this in chapter 4.

The Exception to the Omega 6:3 Rule

Coconuts are the only oily food that break the omega 6:3 rule and are welcome in the balanced raw diet, although still in limited quantities.

Coconut oil should be in a classification of its own because it is an almost entirely saturated fat, containing only omega-6 fatty acids; however, it is one of the healthiest fats we can consume. So what makes coconut oil so special? For one, it is composed of 66 percent medium-chain fatty acids (MCFAs), and MCFAs play a significant role in weight loss, lowering cholesterol, and reducing heart disease. What is even more compelling is MCFAs do not require energy of the liver and gallbladder for digestion, whereas all other fats do. This means when consuming coconut oil, the body has instant energy and an increased metabolic rate, which improves circulation and promotes weight loss.

In addition, other than human breast milk, coconut oil is one of the only food sources that contains lauric acid, which is antiviral, and has been known to inhibit the growth of bacteria and infection in our bodies. Other coconut-containing medium-chain fatty acids have anti-fungal, antibacterial, and antimicrobial properties, and consumption of these fatty acids boosts your immunity. Also, oil derived from coconuts is the only oil that does not break down or denature when heated, making it an acceptable oil to cook with.

EFFICIENT DIGESTION, ASSIMILATION, ABSORPTION, AND ELIMINATION ARE ESSENTIAL

The old adage "You are what you eat" is flawed. It is more accurate to say, "You are what you can break down, absorb, assimilate, and eliminate." Food is the carrier of nutrition, and your digestive system is the highway to health. If you are not eating the right foods, such as those that are enzyme- and mineral-rich, you are not absorbing vital micronutrients, much of the food you eat is not being broken down, and your highway is blocked by a traffic jam.

Lack of nutrients, plus sluggish digestion and stored waste, equal compromised health. Your digestive system must work efficiently for you to reap the nutritional benefits of eating, and you achieve this by eating a diet rich in micro-nutrients and clean, unprocessed food, maintaining healthy gut bacteria, and reducing stress.

Enzymes are important for hundreds of bodily functions, and digestive enzymes are vital to breaking down the food you eat for efficient digestion. This is key! Regardless of how healthful a food is, it will not contribute to good health if you cannot break it down. Without this function, you do not absorb and assimilate your nutrients.

Three key digestive enzymes are *protease*, which digests proteins, *lipase*, which digests fats, and *amylase*, which is responsible for digesting carbohydrates. They break down your food so your body can efficiently absorb and utilize nutrients. According to raw food experts and pioneers David Wolfe and Jenny Ross, the founder of popular raw restaurant 118° in Costa Mesa, California, at temperatures above 118°F (48°C), the strength of the enzymes in food is diminished, the food loses its water content, and the broom-like fibers are softened, keeping them from cleansing your intestines. As stated before, some nutrients require cooking to be more digestible, so here you see again, balance is key.

Another key element of Balanced Raw is the intake of minerals, which must be present to assimilate and absorb enzymes, and certain enzymes are only activated by the presence of minerals. Minerals are hard to come by, as they must be obtained from soil. Our soil is nutrient-deficient because of the use of pesticides and fertilizers. In addition, according to the Food and Agriculture Organization of the United Nations, genetically modified (GM) crops, which make up nearly 85 percent of the American agricultural food supply, can also be nutrient-deficient because of vitamin and mineral content being reduced or altered during GM processing. Dead soil produces dead fruits and vegetables. These foods lack the mineral content necessary to activate enzymes.

To ensure you are consuming sufficiently mineral-rich food, eat plenty of raw, plant-based foods that are grown in organic soil and, whenever possible, are locally sourced. How much is considered plenty? This will vary depending on the person, but ensuring at least 50 percent of your diet is coming from fresh produce will provide you with a good amount of the living enzymes and minerals your body needs to work optimally.

THE BEST SOURCES OF ENZYMES AND MICRONUTRIENTS

Bountiful sources of food enzymes include papaya, avocados, bananas, raw honey, grapes, dates, pineapple, and mangos, and greens such as kale, dandelion, lamb's lettuce (mâche), arugula, Swiss chard, and collards. Also in these foods, as well as all other fruits and vegetables, is an abundance of phytochemicals. *Phyto* means "plant," so *phytochemicals* literally means "plant chemicals." These include antioxidants and are special because they are not present in any other food and are a secret weapon for preventing and reversing chronic disease.

When looking to consume enzyme- and mineral-rich foods, eat those that are suitable for your body. When eating raw, plant-based foods, select those that are easier to digest in their raw form such as lettuces, fennel, radishes, sweet and acid fruits, cucumber, kohlrabi, herbs, sprouts, summer squash, greens such as dandelion and watercress, and celery. Monitor your digestive response when eating raw, hearty greens such as chard, kale, mustard greens, and collards. If you digest them without gas or bloating, you are likely safe to continue eating them this way. If you find eating them raw compromises your digestion, purée them into a smoothie or soup as doing so breaks down the fibers, making them easier to digest.

CHEW YOUR FOOD TO ABSORB AND ASSIMILATE

Most people do not chew their food to the degree necessary for digestive enzyme production, or to efficiently absorb nutrients. Enzymes that break down carbohydrates are first activated in your saliva, and chewing thoroughly aids in digestion by sending signals to your stomach that food is coming and to begin secreting gastric juices that will digest the food. Chewing also allows for enough time for the brain to know when the stomach has been fed enough and to stop eating.

So what does it mean to chew thoroughly? At a minimum, this means you should chew every bite of food at least thirty times before swallowing. There is a wise old saying, "Chew your liquids and drink your solids," so when sipping a smoothie or juice, be sure to chew that, too.

ENJOY A BALANCE OF COOKED AND RAW FOODS FOR OPTIMAL HEALTH AND VITALITY

I know you want me to tell you the exact percentage of raw versus cooked foods to eat, but I simply cannot do that. Someone living in Alaska, for example, may need to consume more warming and cooked foods than a resident of Hawaii. The intent here again is to achieve balance.

But let's do explore why some cooked foods are essential to include. Certain cooked foods, such as beans, grains, tubers, and winter squash, are more digestible. These fibrous foods are more vibrant, tastier, and easier to chew, and their vital nutrients are more bioavailable, meaning an alteration in the cell structure results in digestive enzymes being able to more easily access the nutrients.

The Balanced Raw program encourages you to take in plenty of food enzymes from raw vegetables and fruits, but to provide balance, ensure maximum nutrient assimilation, and eat with the changing seasons, you are encouraged to eat cooked grains, beans, starchy vegetables, and hearty greens.

Take a look at the tomato. A plate of fresh-picked heirlooms sprinkled with basil and drizzled with balsamic vinegar sounds delightful, doesn't it? They are incredibly satisfying to the palate this way, but their powerful antioxidant, *lycopene*, is more bioavailable when cooked with liquid and heat. Maybe the Italians knew something we didn't when they started cooking tomatoes for sauce.

The same is true for red grapes. The skin of the red grape contains a large concentration of *anthocyanins*, potent antioxidants that give grapes their rosy hue. When making wine or grape juice, the crushing action releases these antioxidants into the juice, where they become more digestible.

Beta-carotene, a carotenoid antioxidant that gives carrots and other yellow and orange vegetables and fruits their coloring, is converted into vitamin A by the body, and vitamin A plays a significant role in eye and bone health, brain function, skin clarity, and immune system regulation. Studies show that lightly cooking carrots increases the bioavailability of beta-carotene. The availability of carotenoids in cabbage, asparagus, broccoli, and zucchini are also more abundant when these foods are cooked rather than eaten raw.

SOME COOKING METHODS ARE HEALTHIER THAN OTHERS

Be aware that not all cooking preparations are equal in their health benefits and implications. Baking, frying, and broiling all increase the presence of acrylamide, a cancer-promoting neurotoxin. Acrylamide is produced as a result of carbohydrates being exposed to high heat and for long cook times. Grilling is an acceptable form of cooking as long as you are using gas and not charcoal.

According to a representative at Purdue University and the Physicians Committee for Responsible Medicine, if you are eating meat of any kind, grilling with charcoal increases your risk of cancer. This is because meats produce carcinogenic compounds called heterocyclic amines when cooked at high temperatures. They also produce polycyclic aromatic hydrocarbons, another carcinogen, from the fat being met with charcoal. When the flames flare, they redeposit the carcinogenic molecules back into the meat.

The most desirable cooking processes are steaming, boiling, and simmering. These preparations, especially in the case of steaming, produce vibrant, tender foods, do not require the use of added fat, and ensure more of the nutrients remain intact than in any other cooking process. Also, in the case of certain grains, seeds, and starchy vegetables, steaming destroys harmful antienzymes that interfere with nutrient assimilation. As you destroy these enzyme inhibitors, absorption of nutrients is more efficient and requires less energy and fewer digestive enzymes. A tip for steaming to perfection is to monitor the vibrancy of the food. Dark green broccoli, zucchini, green beans, and pale green asparagus turn bright green when cooked to perfection. Cauliflower, when steamed only a few minutes, will turn slightly translucent when ready to eat, and sweet potatoes will turn brilliant orange when sufficiently steamed.

Vitamin C, which is essential for immune health, is less available when cooked, so vitamin C–containing foods, such as kale, citrus fruits, and parsley, can and should be eaten raw. Healthful ways to consume them include blending them into smoothies and raw soups, and adding them to salads and fresh-pressed juices such as those found in the chapters that follow.

Increase Nutrient Density by Sprouting Your Beans, Grains, and Seeds

Another praised food preparation method is sprouting. The process of soaking and sprouting destroys the anti-enzymes in known foods and reduces digestion time. It also increases the nutritional value because vitamin content is multiplied through the germination process.

To sprout grains, beans, and seeds, you must first soak, or germinate, the food. Germination involves placing the food in fresh water between four and forty-eight hours, depending on which food you are sprouting. Once the food has sufficiently germinated, it is ready to sprout. The steps for sprouting are as follows:

1. Drain soaking water.

2. Give the grain, seed, or bean a good rinse in a fine mesh strainer.

3. Transfer to a wide-mouthed jar, apply a thin layer of cheesecloth over the mouth, and secure with a rubber band.

4. Store the jar in a dark place, such as a cupboard or pantry, and tilt the jar at a 45-degree angle, with the mouth facing downward. Place a kitchen towel under the mouth of the jar to catch any liquid that may leak through.

5. Every six to eight hours, rinse and drain right through the cheesecloth, and then restore the jar to its resting place.

6. Follow the guidelines in the chart below for various sprouting times.

Ferment Foods for a Happy and Healthy Gut

For centuries, cultures have consumed naturally fermented foods at the start of their meal to increase healthy gut flora and ready the digestive system for consumption of cooked and raw foods. Fermented foods are some of the most nutritious foods available,

FOOD	SOAK TIME	SPROUT TIME
Legumes		
Adzuki	12 hours	1 to 2 days
Chickpeas	12 hours	2 days
Lentils	8 hours	2 days
Mung beans	12 hours	2 days
Grains		
Amaranth	4 hours	1 day
Buckwheat	8 hours	2 days
Millet	10 hours	2 days
Quinoa	4 to 6 hours	12 hours
Wild rice	48 hours	1 day—will not yield sprouts, but cracks when ready to eat
Seeds		
Chia	6 hours	3 days
Flax	4 hours	2 days
Sesame	6 hours	1 day (use unhulled seeds)
Sunflower	6 hours	2 days (use hulled seeds)

and Balanced Raw favorites include apple cider vinegar, sauerkraut (fermented cabbage), kimchi, olives, kombucha (fermented tea), and miso (fermented soy or chickpeas). The fermentation process causes bacteria to eat the sugars present in these foods. Digestion of these sugars results in probiotic-rich or gut-friendly bacteria. Fermented vegetables are nutrient dense and full of fiber, contain digestion-enhancing enzymes, and should be eaten at least a couple of times per week as part of the Balanced Raw diet.

CONSUME COOKED AND RAW FOODS AT EVERY MEAL FOR BALANCED NUTRITION

As mentioned, to be Balanced Raw means to eat a healthy ratio of cooked and raw foods. To provide a clear picture of what this might look like, visualize a plate divided into four equal segments. At least two of the quarters will be filled with fresh and raw foods, such as the **Happy Belly Sprout Salad** (page 127) and **Mediterranean Herb Kale Salad** (page 128), and the other 50 percent, or remaining two quadrants, would include nourishing, lightly cooked or steamed foods such as the **Glowing Greens and Hemp Soup** (page 78), and a steamed vegetable such as green beans drizzled with lemon juice and seasoned with sea salt and fresh thyme.

Part of the Balanced Raw diet includes finding your groove with the way you approach this part-time raw lifestyle. To better understand how to do this, you need to understand bio-uniqueness. What is bio-uniqueness, you ask? It is what makes you, you. It is the carefully crafted cocktail that blends your lifestyle, activities, tendencies, likes and dislikes, health conditions, genetic makeup, and habits. It is unfortunate that the dozens of diet and nutrition books that make it to the shelves every year fail to examine the complex makeup of the individual. Rather, they strive to fit millions of biologically unique people into a predefined diet container, leaving no room for even a little flexibility.

To be a Balanced Raw foodist for life, some breathing room is essential because your daily schedule, fitness activities, stress, availability of food, and travel may greatly affect your ability to stay on course. Worry and stress about your diet and whether or not you are following it perfectly will keep you from being in balance and will promote disease.

In the Balanced Raw plan, you are encouraged to listen to your body and pay attention when something feels off. Do not force raw or cooked foods if you find you do not digest them easily, or cannot stand their taste. Allow for a little flexibility and you will be able to remain Balanced Raw for life.

CHAPTER 2

MANAGE YOUR MACRONUTRIENTS FOR A STRONG AND HEALTHY BODY

TRADITIONAL RAW DIETS HAVE TIPPED THE NUTRIENT SCALE, weighed down by too many fats. They also lack macronutrient variety. According to respected medical professionals such as John McDougall, M.D., and T. Colin Campbell, Ph.D., fat consumption should be limited to only 10 percent of your total daily caloric intake, and fats should come from whole food sources, such as olives, seeds, and avocado, and from small amounts of nuts, if at all.

Traditional raw diets have focused on using nuts and oil to create richness, creaminess, and texture in plant-based sauces, desserts, and dressings. However, legumes, healthful seeds, and starchy vegetables can also add decadence to a tart, silkiness to a cream sauce, and increased emulsification for dressings.

ACTUALIZE RICHNESS AND TEXTURE WITHOUT OIL

So just how do you use these other ingredients to achieve the same richness and texture that oil provides? To bring this into view, visualize making a salad. You have chopped up lots of fresh veggies, selected your greens, and perhaps added some chickpeas, cooked quinoa, or steamed beets. Rather than making a traditional dressing of one-third citrus or acid and two-thirds oil, omit the oil and season the citrus or acid with dried or fresh herbs, minced garlic and shallots, sea salt, and fresh cracked pepper. Then, to bring a touch of fat to your fresh meal, garnish with one-fourth of an avocado that has been cut into small cubes. If you prefer a creamy dressing, add the avocado cubes to the other dressing ingredients and purée in a high-speed blender until smooth. The silkiness of the avocado will go a long way toward adding creaminess to the dressing without the use of oil.

When making sauces, experiment with using cooked beans or starchy vegetables to thicken and emulsify. In the case of the **Shaved Roots and Herbed Parsnip Stack** (page 85), I suggest blending cooked parsnips with fresh herbs and garlic for a savory and versatile purée. Other legumes and vegetables that are ideal for sauce and dressing bases are black beans, chickpeas, peas, and cooked cauliflower, parsnips, and sweet potatoes. When used in moderation, hemp, pumpkin, flax, and chia seeds are also excellent for thickening and adding creaminess to your sauces and dressings.

FULL-FLAVORED REDUCED-FAT TIP

Another way to lower fat is to pulse nuts such as pistachios, almonds, Brazil nuts, or walnuts in a spice grinder and then just sprinkle a teaspoon or two on your dish. You will use far less this way, yet still benefit from the added flavor, crunch, and touch of healthy fat.

BE AN 80:10:10 FOODIE FOR DISEASE PREVENTION AND REVERSAL

The Balanced Raw diet encourages an 80:10:10 macro-nutrient ratio, with 80 percent reserved for carbohydrates and 10 percent allocated to both fats and protein. Extensive research conducted by renowned cardiologist Caldwell B. Esselstyn Jr., M.D., showcases a reduction in heart disease, obesity, diabetes, and even the reversal of cancer when this ratio is adhered to.

In addition, this approach appears to be most similar to the diet followed in Asian cultures, where inhabitants have historically lived long and thriving lives. You will see in chapter 4 how Okinawans, the society with the largest number of documented centurions, eat a diet rich in carbo-hydrates, and use fat and protein to enhance a meal as a condiment, and not as the main attraction.

In the provocative 2008 documentary *Eating*, director Mike Anderson interviews experts in health and nutrition such as Esselstyn and Joseph Crowe, M.D., who describe how our ancestors ate a diet rich in carbohydrates and low in fats and protein. Prior to the agricultural revolution, humans survived on an abundance of fresh vegetables, greens, roots, herbs, fruit, protein-containing grains and legumes, minimal game meat, and nuts and seeds in limited quantities. It was only after the agricultural boom that humans began indulging in processed and refined foods and eating concentrated fats such as vegetable oils.

If you think about the foods available to our ancestors, greens, root vegetables, and fruits were most abundant, meat was sparse because of the need to hunt for game, and nuts and seeds were either unavailable or difficult to harvest. Take cashews, for example. Shelling cashews is a time-consuming process that is achieved by using wooden mallets and sometimes wire to extract the kernel from its hard shell. Then the cashew kernel must have its thin resin coating, known as the testa, removed before consumption. This is achieved by heating the kernels until the testa dries and becomes brittle and thus easier to remove. It is essential that those harvesting be protected from the poisonous ivy–like shell oil, which can damage mucous membranes and severely burn the skin. When you consider this lengthy and somewhat risky process, it is unlikely our ancestors were enjoying cashews or any nut by the handful, and neither should we.

CARBS ARE NOT THE ENEMY

As a Balanced Raw foodie you will easily be able to navigate the complex world of carbohydrates, feeling confident about which are most healthful and nourishing to your body.

I am giddy for grains and after you read about how power-fully nutritious and versatile they are, my hope is that you will be, too. There are so many varieties of these glorious morsels, and the dishes that can be made using these gems are endless. Here are some examples:

Quinoa (pronounced keen-wah), a grain native to the Andes, literally means "the mother of all grains" in the Incan language. Quinoa has been a sacred crop of South American inhabitants for centuries. It has superior digest-ibility, a high protein content, and a full amino acid pro-file—it contains all eight essentials acids that your body does not manufacture. It is a mainstay of many South American meals just as rice is of Asian fare. This light and gluten-free grain is technically a seed and a relative of spinach and beets. In addition to being enjoyed as a side or main dish, cooked quinoa can replace oats or cracked wheat in breakfast porridge, may be tossed with fruits, vegetables, or legumes in a grain salad, can be ground into flour for baked goods, or be used to add texture and volume to a veggie burger. You will soon experience the nutty taste and health qualities of quinoa because it is used in a number of dishes included in this plan.

Millet is another hailed, grain-like seed and is indigenous to India, Africa, and the semiarid tropics of Asia. This gluten-free carbohydrate, with a polenta-like flavor, is rich in fiber and important minerals such as magnesium and phosphorus. Magnesium is essential for healthy bowel function and heart health, and has been shown to contribute to the reduction of high blood pressure. Phosphorus contributes to bone and tissue growth and repair. To enjoy this healthful grain, use cooked millet as an alternative to rice in risottos, for added texture in soups and stews, or for stuffing bell peppers and winter squashes. Introduce your palate to the wonderful texture and mild flavor of millet in the **Fiesta Millet Salad with Smoky Avocado Cream** (page 152).

Keeping with the theme of "seeds as grains," **buckwheat** is another adored carbohydrate. In a report written for the Whole Grains Council in 2004, Rui Hai Liu, M.D., Ph.D., from Cornell University describes how the phytochemical and antioxidant profile of buckwheat reduces your risk of heart disease and diabetes. You can find buckwheat noodles at Asian or health markets, and raw buckwheat groats or kasha (roasted buckwheat) in the bulk aisle of your natural food store. Both the groats and the kasha make a delicious base for hot or cold breakfast cereal, and buckwheat noodles are silky and delightfully slurpable when added to brothy soups or tossed in cold noodle salads. In chapter 6 is a spicy **Thai Buckwheat Noodle Soup** (page 148) that will welcome buckwheat to your carbohydrate repertoire, while warming you to the core.

Last, but no less worthy, is **rice**. There are hundreds of varieties of rice, and in the balanced raw diet you are encouraged to enjoy those with the richest antioxidant, fiber, and protein contents. Those most notable are red rice, also known as Bhutanese rice; black rice, which is sometimes referred to as "forbidden" rice; and long-grain brown rice. Until now, you may have only considered rice to be a lunch or dinnertime grain, but you can also use it in morning porridge and desserts.

EAT STARCHY VEGGIES FOR A HAPPY AND HEALTHY BELLY

Beets, sweet potatoes, parsnips, pumpkin—what do these hearty and fibrous vegetables have in common? These roots, gourds, and tubers are good for your gut and will become new food friends as you adopt the Balanced Raw way of life. These complex carbohydrates are fiber dense, contain plant-based proteins and an abundance of vitamins and antioxidants, and fill you up without needing to eat in excess to feel sated. They also aid in keeping your bowel movements regular, which is essential to good health. In addition, they have a warming effect when cooked, helping you feel nourished and grounded.

Some of my favorite ways to enjoy starchy veggies are in puréed soups, such as the **Celery Root and Leek Soup with Green Apple** (page 77) or as an alternative to grains in the **Parsnip Rice Sushi with Sweet Tamarind Dipping Sauce** (page 171). I also love to dehydrate roots to make homemade chips like the **Za'atar Crusted Parsnip Chips** (page 163).

Get to the Root of Vegetables for Disease Prevention and Energy

If you think about it, root vegetables are very special. They grow beneath the ground, tucked snug in the dirt, where they absorb large amounts of nutrients from the soil. Their leaves are rich in phytochemicals and other nutrient compounds because of the minerals and vitamins making their way up from the roots and from the photosynthesis of the sun. For this reason, be sure to include leafy greens in your diet, too! For example, add beet greens to your **Ruby Rabbit Pressed Juice** (page 113) for a mega dose of phytochemical love.

Roots are a complex carbohydrate and turn to sugar in the body, giving you sustained energy. The fiber in the roots slows the sugar uptake, helping you feel sated and full longer. Despite their sweet taste, they are very low in calories, making them ideal for consumption if you are watching your weight. Roots are known to have an abundance of beta-carotene, magnesium, and potassium, and all of these nutrients boost the immune system, reduce inflammation, nourish your organs, and prevent life-threatening diseases such as cancer, stroke, diabetes, and heart disease.

THE GREAT PROTEIN DEBATE

I am sure you have heard before that raw, vegan, and vegetarian diets lack protein; however, that theory is fast being debunked. Most humans, whether rawtarians or not, consume sufficient amounts of protein because our bodies do not require as much as once thought, and the kinds of amino acids (the building blocks of protein) we consume are far more critical than the number of protein grams eaten in a given day.

In an article titled "Protein and Amino Acid Requirements in Human Nutrition," distributed by the World Health Organization in 2002, researchers describe how an adequate intake of protein for humans is only 10 percent or less of total calories consumed per day. This percentage may be a few points lower if you have a less active lifestyle.

A great misconception is that plant proteins are inferior to animal sources because meat proteins contain all amino acids in a single source. Contrary to years of this thinking, eating large amounts of protein from animal sources is not ideal for human consumption. Amino acids found in meat are bound into complex combinations of long-chain amino acids, and these long molecule chains must first be broken down by hydrochloric (stomach) acid and enzymes to be absorbed. This is a time-consuming process and a poor use of energy, which results in lethargy and keeps our precious energy reserves from being used for other vital bodily functions.

WHY PLANT PROTEINS ARE SUPERIOR

The amino acid composition of plants is characterized by individual, short-chain amino acids that are more bio-available, or ready for absorption, which you learned in chapter 1 is essential to exceptional health. Also, your body only requires that the eight essential amino acids (those you do not naturally manufacture) come from the food you eat while you produce the other twelve that are required for good health. Plant proteins contain all eight amino acids, and, in most cases, in a short-chain structure, which is ideal. The intake of individual acids keeps the digestive system from being burdened with the task of breaking apart complex and tangled chains prior to assimilation.

Your body also does not require all eight amino acids to be present in a single meal. As long as you are consuming individual amino acids throughout the day, your body will know how best to use them. To ensure you are getting all essential amino acids variety is key, and you do this in the Balanced Raw diet by consuming a bounty of vegetables and fruits as well as cooked grains, legumes, and seeds.

In fact, you may be surprised, but there is actually more protein in certain plant foods, calorie for calorie, than in beef. Highly regarded hemp seeds, for example, are made up of 50 percent protein, quinoa weighs in at 17 percent, and a whopping one-third of spinach is protein!

LOOK TO THE SEA FOR PROTEIN POWER

Believe it or not, sea vegetables are one of the most protein-dense plant food sources known to humans. In thriving Asian nations, seaweed and algae are part of nearly every meal, including rice and noodle dishes, soups, stews, and salads. They also enjoy dried and seasoned seaweed as a light snack. If you are not yet familiar with these nutritious water foods, here is a list of these highly regarded protein powerhouses:

Spirulina is a blue-green algae that contains high concentrations of B vitamins, beta-carotene, iron, and antioxidants, and provides more than one hundred minerals and vitamins. This buttery- and grassy-flavored sea green has an astonishing amount of protein, with between 55 and 70 percent of its calories coming from amino acids, depending on the variety. Spirulina also contains all essential amino acids in short chains for easy assimilation. Look for spirulina in powdered form at your health food store and add it to smoothies and desserts, sprinkle on vegetable chips and salads, add to dressings such as the one found in the

Big Herb Salad with Creamy Garlic and Spirulina Dressing (page 69), or stir into soups and stews.

Nori is a Japanese seaweed that is nutty in flavor and found in dried sheets at any health food or Asian market. Nori is comprised of one-third protein and is abundant in fiber. To incorporate it into your diet, grind nori for sprinkling, or use the sheets as wrappers and fill with vegetables, rice, mashed roots, or legumes.

Hijiki is brown algae that has a rich salty flavor, is 10 percent protein, and is packed with fiber. It contains plentiful amounts of potassium, magnesium, iron, and calcium, and is scrumptious when added to broth soups, sprinkled on salads, included in wraps, or sprinkled atop a bowl of grains, vegetables, and legumes.

Chlorella is a single-celled green algae, rich in vitamins, minerals, and omega-3 fatty acids, and contains 50 percent protein. Chlorella can be purchased in powdered form or tablets, and its earthy and nutty flavor is a welcome addition to smoothies and green drinks, or simply eaten in its raw form.

SHOW SOME LOVE FOR LEGUMES AND FEEL NOURISHED IN RETURN

For so long, legumes have had a somewhat negative, if not entirely bad rap, being referred to as nature's "oops" because they contain both starch and protein in a single source. The argument is that the presence of these two macronutrients in the same environment is responsible for digestive unrest, diarrhea, gas, and bloating.

These uncomfortable symptoms can, and do, result from improper preparation of legumes, so to ensure you are eating the finest, most digestible, and most nutritional legumes, follow these recommendations:

1. Try not to buy or eat canned beans. They often contain preservatives and excess sodium, have not been degassed, and have trace amounts of aluminum from the can, which is destructive to good health.

2. Try to purchase only whole, dried, and organic legumes.

3. Always examine them for rocks and other foreign particles, and then rinse thoroughly in a colander. Next, soak, or germinate, the legumes in fresh water, ensuring they are covered with four times their amount in water. Let rest at room temperature for at least 12 hours and ideally 24 to help them predigest and release their gas-promoting elements.

4. After soaking, the legumes should be rinsed thoroughly with clean water. Transfer them to a large soup pot, cover with an extra 2 inches (5.1 cm) of fresh water, and bring to a low boil.

5. Once boiling, turn the heat to medium-low and simmer uncovered until cooked through. Cooking times can range from 30 minutes to 1 hour depending on the bean. Sample every 15 minutes to check for doneness, and pull from the heat once they have just a slight bite. Perfectly cooked legumes will not be mushy.

6. Drain the cooking water (or reserve to thin sauces and dressings) and then season the legumes with herbs and spices such as thyme, bay leaves, oregano, salt, cumin, black pepper, ginger, or chili powder. Aromatics and vegetables such as celery, onions, garlic, and carrots can be added during simmering to enhance flavor.

7. Use legumes immediately, refrigerate, or freeze for future use in any meal such as burgers, chili, stews, salads, wraps, casseroles, sauces, and dressings.

Following these guidelines will reduce digestive discomfort and will encourage you to enjoy the many healthy benefits of these tasty gems. With each serving, you get a provocative protein profile, plenty of fiber, and an abundance of vitamins and minerals, all in a versatile, convenient, and savory Balanced Raw–friendly food.

CHAPTER 3

PREPARE YOUR BODY, KITCHEN, AND MIND FOR THE BALANCED RAW PLAN

THROUGHOUT YOUR LIFE, HOW MANY TIMES HAVE YOU LAID THE FOUNDATION FOR SOMETHING NEW? Perhaps you have role-played for an upcoming interview, enrolled in classes to pursue a specific career, taken lessons to learn how to play an instrument, or started training in preparation for a race. You may not even realize all the foundation building you have been doing to support the weight of demanding tasks, goals, and responsibilities.

Adopting a sustainable Balanced Raw lifestyle is no different from these other endeavors and also requires a firm and steady foundation. This foundation includes a pantry that is free of junk and instead stocked with foods that nourish and support your health goals; kitchen tools and equipment that make Balanced Raw meal prep a breeze; a support system of people who encourage and keep you motivated; and most important, a clear intention about why you desire to live this way.

WITHOUT A SOLID FOUNDATION, YOUR COMMITMENT MAY BECOME WEAKENED and your dedication can lose its oomph. You have likely seen examples of this in the first month or so of each new year. The new year typically starts with an explosive rise in gym memberships, diets, workout programs, and sky-rocketing sales of get-thin-quick pills. Millions are suddenly dedicated to losing weight, giving up their smoking habit, saving more money, or being more kind and loving to their spouse or children. But then what happens? Why, after only a few weeks or months, are commitments broken and dedication diminished? Why do the once devoted give up?

More often than not, it is not because these devotees want to fail at achieving their goals; most really do want to be slim, smoke-free, and more loving. What makes them give up is a weak or nonexistent foundation. It happens when the person committed to losing weight signs up for the gym or purchases a weight loss supplement but does not eliminate junk food from his pantry. It happens when a lover or spouse sets a goal to be more kind and loving but fails to forgive hurts from the past or fails to learn how to communicate and show love in the way her child or spouse will best receive it.

ESTABLISH AN INDESTRUCTIBLE INTENTION FOR ADHERING TO THE BALANCED RAW PROGRAM

A stable foundation and clear intention are the keys to success when altering your lifestyle for the better. Have you stopped to consider why you are committing to this four-week program? Is it for weight loss? Are you an athlete looking to achieve peak performance? Do you want to finally be free of digestive pain, headaches, insomnia, or allergies? Are you fed up with battling diabetes, heart disease, or chronic fatigue? Have you "tried everything, but nothing has seemed to work"?

Whatever your purpose is for following the Balanced Raw system, put pen to paper and clearly define your intention. Display this written reminder promi-nently on your refrigerator, computer, bathroom mirror, or anywhere you will see it throughout the day. You can even set an alert on your cell phone to remind you each day of your purpose for choosing the Balanced Raw way.

The support system I spoke of earlier is essential for building a firm foundation. Maybe you will turn to a spouse for support, or a caring friend. Consider joining a Meetup group in your area whose focus is on health and wellness. These local groups host potlucks, seminars, and other gatherings and get you rubbing shoulders with some people who may be making a similar transition or are already living the Balanced Raw way. Being around like-minded people, or engaging those nearest to your heart to keep you motivated and on track, will ease you through the changes. If you feel safe and comfortable doing so, speak freely about the physical, mental, and emotional changes. Share your goals and milestones and ask for help when needed.

With a clear intention and a supportive network, you can begin building the foundation that will serve you during this transition and set you up for success in achieving your goals.

THE FIRST LAYER OF YOUR FOUNDATION: PREP THE PANTRY AND CONDITION THE KITCHEN

In the next chapter, you will give your kitchen a complete makeover—a healthy overhaul, if you will. Your refrigerator, freezer, and pantry will be stripped of all garbage food that brings harm to your body and will be restocked with an abundance of nourishing, whole, and natural foods to enjoy in your home cooking. You won't feel deprived after learning how incredibly tasty and satisfying whole and natural foods can be.

Have you ever gone to the store and picked up a bag of brightly speckled beans or colorful rice you had not seen before only to get it home, put it in your pantry, and completely forget about it? If so, you are not the only one. Many do this with the intent to prepare the new food, but without it prominently displayed, and without some

guidelines for preparation, it could end up living for years in your cupboard completely neglected. Part of the process of building your foundation includes storing and displaying your foods in a way that makes them more appealing and appetizing, and that puts them front and center so you are more likely to eat them. Decoratively display the jars of dried, whole foods in your pantry and refrigerator and on countertops so they stare back at you, enticing you to eat them up.

You should also begin to shop the bulk aisles of your markets for dried goods such as grains, legumes, seeds, fruits, flour, and spices. Buying from bulk bins saves you money and encourages you to either purchase large quantities if you have the storage to do so, or smaller quantities more frequently while still reaping the benefits of bulk pricing. Following are some key dried ingredients you will want to have on hand.

LEGUMES

Legumes are perfect for the Balanced Raw diet, and some of the most common and included in the following recipes are French green lentils, black beluga lentils, red lentils, dried garbanzo beans (chickpeas), dried Northern white beans, dried adzuki beans, dried black beans, and split peas.

All of these tasty beauties can be used in a variety of ways, from adding them to soups and stews to making veggie burgers, stuffing bell peppers and squash, and puréeing into sauces, dressings, dips, and spreads. You can also sprinkle cooked legumes on salads or over a bowl of steamed vegetables and cooked grains.

GRAINS AND RICE

Additional perfect pantry staples are bulk raw grains. Grains are incredibly versatile and as you learned in chapter 2, the ones that are the most healthful are those that are gluten-free and protein- and fiber-rich. Here is a list of these grains and cooking instructions:

Raw buckwheat groats: Soak 2 cups groats in cold water overnight. Strain off soaking water in the morning and rinse thoroughly until water runs clear and all silkiness is removed. Sprout using the guidelines in chapter 1 and then enjoy whole or blend with ingredients such as cinnamon, nutmeg, cacao powder, vanilla, maple syrup, or agave for a delightful and nourishing breakfast cereal.

Millet: Use a ratio of 1 cup millet to $2^1/_2$ cups water. Bring water to a boil, add millet, cover, and simmer for 25 minutes. Remove from heat, fluff with a fork, and let millet sit uncovered for an additional 5 to 10 minutes, or until desired texture has been achieved.

Quinoa (black, red, white): Rinse thoroughly in a fine mesh strainer prior to cooking. Use a ratio of 1 cup quinoa to 2 cups water. Bring water to a boil, add quinoa, cover, and simmer for 12 minutes. Remove lid and fluff with a fork.

Amaranth: Use a ratio of 1 cup amaranth to 3 cups water. Bring water to a boil, add amaranth, cover, and simmer for 25 to 30 minutes. Remove lid and fluff with a fork.

Red rice: Rinse thoroughly prior to cooking. Use a ratio of 1 cup red rice to 2 cups water. Bring water to a boil, then add rice, cover, and simmer for 40 to 45 minutes. Remove from heat and fluff with a fork.

Black rice: Rinse thoroughly prior to cooking. Use a ratio of 1 cup black rice to 2 cups water. Bring water to a boil, add rice, cover, and simmer for 30 to 35 minutes. Remove lid and let simmer, uncovered, for 5 to 10 minutes more, or until desired texture has been achieved. Fluff with a fork.

Brown rice: Rinse thoroughly in cold water prior to cooking. Use a ratio of 1 cup brown rice to $2^1/_2$ cups water. Add both rice and water to saucepan and bring to a boil. Reduce heat to low, cover, and simmer for 40 minutes. Remove from heat, and let stand, covered, for an additional 15 minutes. Remove lid and fluff with a fork.

Wild rice: Rinse thoroughly prior to cooking. Use a ratio of 1 cup wild rice to $3^1/_2$ cups water. Add both rice and water to saucepan and bring to a boil. Reduce heat to low, cover, and simmer for 50 minutes. Uncover and simmer with lid removed for an additional 5 to 10 minutes until all liquid has evaporated.

FLAVOR YOUR FOOD WITH SEASONINGS, HERBS, AND SPICES

Including herbs and spices in meal prep is your secret weapon to full-flavored cuisine. They add dimension, savor, and complexity without the need for fat and other additives. Restock your dried seasonings, herbs, and spices every six months to ensure freshness and strength in flavor. Ideally, you will want to purchase organic spices in small quantities and from your bulk aisle. Common spices you will use in the books recipes and in your new Balanced Raw lifestyle include: bay leaf, sea salt, ground cumin, cumin seed, caraway seed, coriander seed, ground turmeric, ground ginger, ground coriander, black pepper, white pepper, chili powder, cayenne pepper, curry powder, dried thyme, dried oregano, dried basil, dried marjoram, dried tarragon, garlic powder, pumpkin pie spice, ground clove, ground sage, ground chipotle powder, ground cinnamon, and ground nutmeg.

FLOURS, GROUND MEALS, AND DRIED SPECIALTY ITEMS

Alkalizing and gluten-free meals and flours are also valuable additions to your pantry and can be used to make pancakes, thicken a sauce, and add bulk and texture to sweet treats such as the **Body-Loving Lemon Bars** (page 164). Balanced Raw favorites include quinoa flour, coconut flour, garbanzo bean (chickpea) flour, buckwheat flour, almond meal, teff flour, brown rice flour, and flax meal (ground flaxseeds).

In addition, there are a few dried specialty items you will want to have on hand and that the following recipes call for. These include:

Raw cacao powder: This nutrient powerhouse contains sixty-six antioxidants and is ideal for desserts, smoothies, shakes, and puddings.

Nutritional yeast: This inactive yeast has a cheesy flavor, making it an excellent addition to sauces and dressings. Nutritional yeast should not be confused with that found in baked goods because it does not instigate rise or promote expansion and elasticity. This yeast generally does not trigger allergies or other immune responses, is rich in B vitamins, and is easy to digest.

Unsweetened shredded coconut: Full of medium-chain fatty acids, it adds rich flavor to desserts, porridge and other breakfast foods, and smoothies.

Dates: You may be surprised that this sugary dried fruit has an abundance of fiber, enzymes, potassium, and iron. And because of its high fructose content, all you need is just one or two dates when blending into smoothies and desserts to enhance their sweetness.

Sun-dried tomatoes: When tomatoes have been sun-dried, they become more salty, turn a bit musky, and develop a very robust flavor. Blend into soups, dressings, and sauces for added dimension or chop and add to wraps and pizza. You can also grind very dry sun-dried tomatoes into a powder to add a pinch here and there.

Dried seaweeds: Dried dulse, nori, arame, hijiki, and wakame are excellent for adding to soups, grinding to sprinkle on salads, and using as wraps for sushi and veggie rolls.

FORTIFY YOUR REFRIGERATOR

Whenever you shop your natural foods store or farmers' market, make a habit of coming right home and prepping your produce for consumption within the coming days and storing properly for lasting freshness. The chart on the next pages outlines how to prep and store seventy common produce items so you can avoid wasting product as well as have healthful and ready-to-eat snacks on hand.

FOOD	REFRIGERATE OR ROOM TEMPERATURE	DAYS TO REMAIN FRESH IF UNPREPPED	HOW TO PREP	HOW TO STORE IF NOT PREPPED
Apples	Refrigerate	2 weeks	Wash and cut into segments, and drizzle with fresh lemon juice to keep from discoloring. Store in airtight glass and juice, blend, or snack on them for up to 3 days after cutting.	Store loose in crisper drawer of refrigerator.
Artichokes	Refrigerate	1 week	Do not wash or cut until ready to use. To cook, trim spiny leaves, wash, and steam for 1 hour. You can finish on the grill for 15 minutes for added flavor and texture.	Drape with a damp cloth and store in an airtight container in main compartment or crisper of refrigerator.
Arugula	Refrigerate	2 days	Wash and dry thoroughly. Use within 2 days.	Wrap with a dry towel and store in an open container. Do not store near melons, stone fruits, tomatoes, figs, bananas, or apples.
Asparagus	Room temperature	3 to 5 days	Wash, trim, and steam for 2 minutes. Store in airtight glass for up to 2 days.	Store upright in a bowl or glass with the bases resting in a small amount of water.
Avocado	Paper bag at room temperature	3–4 days once ripe	If you cut, wrap the unused portion immediately with plastic wrap and store in the main compartment of the refrigerator. Do not store in crisper drawer.	If unripe, store in a paper bag at room temperature. If ripe, store at room temperature in the open air.
Bananas	Room temperature	2 to 3 days once ripe	Peel and freeze or add fresh to smoothies.	Store on countertop in well-ventilated area.
Basil	Room temperature	1 week	Wash and dry thoroughly and use to blend into pesto, add to soups and salads, or to add dimension to fresh pressed juices.	Store at room temperature in a glass with a small amount of water for stems to soak in. Remove any leaves that are wilting and discolored.
Beets	Refrigerate	4 weeks	Use fresh for juicing, or peel and steam for 15 minutes. Cube and store in airtight glass for salads, etc.	Cut greens off and leave 1 inch (2.5 cm) of stem. Brush off all dirt but do not wash until ready to cook. Cover with damp towel and store in open container.
Bell peppers	Refrigerate	3 to 5 days	Do not wash until ready for use.	Store loose in crisper. Do not store near melons, stone fruits, tomatoes, figs, bananas, or apples.

FOOD	REFRIGERATE OR ROOM TEMPERATURE	DAYS TO REMAIN FRESH IF UNPREPPED	HOW TO PREP	HOW TO STORE IF NOT PREPPED
Blackberries	Refrigerate	3 to 5 days	Do not wash until ready to use. Juice, blend, or add to salads and cereal. May wash and dry thoroughly and freeze immediately for future use.	Store unwashed in a paper bag in main compartment of refrigerator. Do not store in crisper drawer.
Blueberries	Refrigerate	3 to 5 days	Do not wash until ready to use. Juice, blend, or add to salads and cereal. May wash and dry thoroughly and freeze immediately for future use.	Store unwashed in a paper bag in main compartment of refrigerator. Do not store in crisper drawer.
Broccoli	Refrigerate	5 days	Wash and break off florets. Use to juice or steam for 1 to 2 minutes. Rinse with cold water, dry, and store in airtight glass for use within 2 to 3 days.	Do not wash. Wrap with a damp towel and store in an open container in the main compartment of refrigerator. Do not store near melons, stone fruits, tomatoes, figs, bananas, or apples.
Brussels sprouts	Refrigerate	1 to 2 weeks	Trim away damaged leaves, wash, and steam for 5 to 7 minutes or until bright green. Run under cool water, dry thoroughly, and store in airtight glass for use within 2 to 3 days.	Trim away damaged leaves and store in an open container lightly draped with a damp towel. Do not store near melons, stone fruits, tomatoes, figs, bananas, or apples.
Cabbage	Refrigerate	1 week	Shred and store in airtight glass. Use within 2 to 3 days.	Store in crisper. Peel off wilting leaves. Do not store near melons, stone fruits, tomatoes, figs, bananas, or apples.
Carrots	Refrigerate	1 to 2 weeks	Peel, cut, and steam for 2 to 3 minutes or peel and cut into strips for snacking. May also grate or julienne cut for salads, bowls, and wraps. Use within 3 days after cutting.	Remove greens and wrap in a damp towel and then store loosely in a produce bag in the crisper. Do not store near melons, stone fruits, tomatoes, figs, bananas, or apples.
Cauliflower	Refrigerate	7 days	Break off florets, wash, and steam for 2 minutes. Store in airtight glass for up to 2 days.	Do not wash unless using right away. Store in main compartment of refrigerator. Do not store near melons, stone fruits, tomatoes, figs, bananas, or apples.
Celery	Room temperature or refrigerate	7 days	Wash and cut into strips for snacking or juicing and store in a shallow, open container submerged in water. Use within 2 to 3 days once cut.	Place bases in a little bit of water and store on countertop or wrap with a damp cloth and store in crisper drawer of refrigerator.

FOOD	REFRIGERATE OR ROOM TEMPERATURE	DAYS TO REMAIN FRESH IF UNPREPPED	HOW TO PREP	HOW TO STORE IF NOT PREPPED
Celery root	Refrigerate	2 weeks	Do not cut until ready to use. Steam for 8 minutes and purée.	Wrap in a damp towel and store in crisper drawer.
Cherries	Refrigerate	5 days	Do not wash until ready to use. Juice, blend, or add to salads and cereal. May wash and dry thoroughly, pit, and freeze immediately.	Store unwashed in a paper bag in main compartment of refrigerator. Do not store in crisper drawer.
Cilantro	Refrigerate	5 days	Keep leaves attached to stems. Wash and dry thoroughly.	Store in a loose, fabric produce bag with a dry paper towel inside to absorb excess moisture. Store in main compartment of refrigerator and not in crisper drawer.
Corn	Refrigerate	3 to 4 days	Husk, wash, and then boil corn for 7 minutes. Remove corn kernels to toss into salads or blend into soups.	Store unhusked in uncovered glass container in main compartment of refrigerator. Do not store in crisper drawer.
Cucumbers	Room temperature or refrigerate	3 days at room temperature or 5 days refrigerated	Peel or scrub and slice into disks and sticks for snacking or use for juicing. Once cut, enjoy within 2 days.	Store on countertop in cool place or in the main compartment of refrigerator. Do not store in crisper and do not store near melons, stone fruits, tomatoes, figs, bananas, or apples.
Dandelion greens	Refrigerate	2 days	Do not wash until ready to use. Add to salads or juice the leaves.	Store loose in an open container in the crisper. Do not store near melons, stone fruits, tomatoes, figs, bananas, or apples.
Dill	Refrigerate	5 days	Keep leaves attached to stems. Wash and dry thoroughly.	Store in the container it came in or store in a loose, fabric produce bag with a dry paper towel inside to absorb excess moisture. Store in main compartment of refrigerator.
Eggplant	Room temperature	1 week	Do not cut until ready to use.	Store unwashed at room temperature in a cool, dry, and well-ventilated place. Do not store near melons, stone fruits, tomatoes, figs, bananas, or apples.
Fennel	Room temperature or refrigerate	2 to 3 days at room temperature or 1 week refrigerated	Scrub clean and shave into thin strips for salads.	Allow base to rest in a shallow dish with a small amount of water. Use within 2 to 3 days or refrigerate, wrapping in a damp towel and storing in crisper drawer.

FOOD	REFRIGERATE OR ROOM TEMPERATURE	DAYS TO REMAIN FRESH IF UNPREPPED	HOW TO PREP	HOW TO STORE IF NOT PREPPED
Figs	Refrigerate	5 to 7 days	Do not wash or cut until ready to use.	Store in a paper bag in main compartment of refrigerator. Do not store in crisper drawer.
Garlic	Room temperature or refrigerate	2 weeks	Peel and store in a dark, airtight glass jar in refrigerator. Use within 5 to 7 days once peeled.	Store unpeeled in a cool, dry, and dark place.
Ginger	Refrigerate	2 weeks	Do not peel until ready to use. Juice whole or add peeled and cut ginger to soups, dressings, sauces, and smoothies.	Wrap loosely in a damp paper towel and store in crisper drawer.
Grapefruit	Room temperature	1 week	Do not cut until ready to use. Refrigerate for 1 to 2 days prior to juicing for best flavor.	Store on countertop in a cool, well-ventilated area.
Grapes	Refrigerate	3 to 5 days	Do not wash until ready to use. Add to salads or juice. Freeze washed grapes for a refreshing treat.	Store in a fabric produce bag in main compartment of refrigerator. Do not store in crisper drawer.
Green beans	Refrigerate	1 week	Wash and trim. Steam for 1 minute and then rinse with cold water. Dry thoroughly and enjoy as a snack or cut up for salads. Store in airtight glass and use within 2 to 3 days after steaming. You may also freeze them.	Wrap in a damp towel and store in crisper drawer.
Kale	Refrigerate	5 days	Do not wash until ready to use. Add to salads, juice, or blend into smoothies and soups.	Store in a fabric produce bag with a dry paper towel and in the main compartment of your refrigerator. Do not store near melons, stone fruits, tomatoes, figs, bananas, or apples.
Kiwi	Refrigerate	5 to 7 days	Peel and cut into segments and store in airtight glass. Enjoy cut fruit within 2 days.	Store uncut kiwi loose in crisper drawer.
Kohlrabi	Refrigerate	1 week	Peel and cut into strips or shave thin. Add to salads or eat as a snack. Enjoy within 3 days once cut.	Store in an open container in main compartment of refrigerator. Do not store in crisper drawer.
Leeks	Refrigerate	7 days	Do not wash until ready to use.	Wrap in a damp towel and store in crisper drawer.

FOOD	REFRIGERATE OR ROOM TEMPERATURE	DAYS TO REMAIN FRESH IF UNPREPPED	HOW TO PREP	HOW TO STORE IF NOT PREPPED
Lemons	Room temperature	1 week	Do not cut until ready to use. Refrigerate for 1 to 2 days prior to juicing for best flavor.	Store on countertop in a cool, well-ventilated area.
Limes	Room temperature	1 week	Do not cut until ready to use. Refrigerate for 1 to 2 days prior to juicing for best flavor.	Store on countertop in a cool, well-ventilated area.
Mâche (lamb's lettuce)	Refrigerate	1 week	Wash and dry thoroughly. Use for salads and juicing.	Store in a loose, fabric produce bag with a dry paper towel and in the main compartment of refrigerator. Do not store in crisper drawer.
Mango	Room temperature until ripe	5 to 7 days	Peel and cut into strips for snacking or to add to smoothies. May also be frozen. Enjoy within 3 days of cutting.	Store in a cool, dry, and well-ventilated place. Once ripe, store loose in crisper drawer.
Melon	Room temperature until ripe	5 to 7 days	Peel and then slice or cube and store in airtight glass. Enjoy blended into smoothies, juiced, or eaten whole within 2 to 3 days of cutting.	Ripen at room temperature and then store in main compartment of refrigerator.
Mint	Refrigerate	5 days	Keep leaves attached to stems. Wash and dry thoroughly.	Store in a loose, fabric produce bag with a dry paper towel inside to absorb excess moisture. Store in main compartment of refrigerator. Do not store in crisper drawer.
Mixed greens	Refrigerate	2 days	Do not wash until ready for use. Add to salads.	Store loose in an open container in the crisper drawer of refrigerator. Do not store near melons, stone fruits, tomatoes, figs, bananas, or apples.
Mushrooms	Refrigerate	5 to 7 days	Do not wash until ready for use and only clean with a damp towel or mushroom brush. Never fully submerge in water. You may also dehydrate for longer storage.	Store in a paper bag in main compartment of refrigerator. Do not store in crisper.
Nectarines	Room temperature until ripe	5 to 7 days	Wash and cut into segments and store in airtight glass to enjoy as a snack or to add to smoothies and salads within 3 days of cutting.	Store in a cool, dry, and well-ventilated place. Once ripe, store loose in your crisper drawer.

FOOD	REFRIGERATE OR ROOM TEMPERATURE	DAYS TO REMAIN FRESH IF UNPREPPED	HOW TO PREP	HOW TO STORE IF NOT PREPPED
Onions	Room temperature	2 to 3 weeks	Do not cut until ready to use.	Store in a cool, dark, dry, and well-ventilated place.
Oranges	Room temperature	1 week	Do not cut until ready to use. Refrigerate for 1 to 2 days prior to juicing for best flavor.	Store on countertop in a cool, well-ventilated area.
Parsley	Refrigerate	5 days	Keep leaves attached to stems. Wash and dry thoroughly.	Store in a loose, fabric produce bag with a dry paper towel inside to absorb excess moisture. Store in main compartment of refrigerator. Do not store near melons, stone fruits, tomatoes, figs, bananas, or apples.
Parsnips	Refrigerate	2 weeks	Peel, cube, and steam for 10 minutes. Store in airtight glass and enjoy within 3 days.	Wash and wrap with a damp towel and store in your crisper drawer.
Peaches	Room temperature until ripe	5 to 7 days	Wash and cut into segments and store in airtight glass to enjoy as a snack or to add to smoothies and salads within 3 days of cutting.	Store in a cool, dry, and well-ventilated place. Once ripe, store loose in your crisper drawer.
Pears	Room temperature	2 weeks	Do not cut until ready to use.	Store on countertop in a cool, ventilated area or in crisper drawer of refrigerator.
Peppers, chiles	Refrigerate	1 week	Do not cut until ready to use unless you wish to wash, cut, and freeze immediately.	Store in paper bag in the crisper drawer. Do not store near melons, stone fruits, tomatoes, figs, bananas, or apples.
Pineapple	Room temperature until ripe	5 to 7 days	Peel and then slice or cube and store in airtight glass. Enjoy blended into smoothies, juiced, or eaten whole within 2 to 3 days of cutting.	Ripen at room temperature, then store in main compartment of refrigerator. Loosely wrap in fabric produce bag.
Potatoes	Room temperature	2 months	Do not peel until ready to use.	Store in a cool, dark, and dry place or paper bag.
Radishes	Refrigerate	2 weeks	Cut away greens and wash to be eaten whole or juiced.	Remove greens and store in an open container in the main compartment of refrigerator covered with a damp towel.
Raspberries	Refrigerate	3 to 5 days	Do not wash until ready to use. Juice, blend, or add to salads and cereal. You may wash and dry thoroughly and freeze immediately.	Store unwashed in paper bag in main compartment of refrigerator. Do not store in crisper drawer.

FOOD	REFRIGERATE OR ROOM TEMPERATURE	DAYS TO REMAIN FRESH IF UNPREPPED	HOW TO PREP	HOW TO STORE IF NOT PREPPED
Romaine	Refrigerate	2 to 3 days	Wash and dry thoroughly. Add to smoothies and juices or use for salads.	Store in a fabric bag with a dry paper towel and in the main compartment of refrigerator. Do not store near melons, stone fruits, tomatoes, figs, bananas, or apples.
Rutabagas	Refrigerate	2 weeks	Peel, cube, and steam for 15 minutes. Store in airtight glass for use within 3 to 4 days after cooking.	Store unwashed in a closed glass container in the crisper drawer.
Scallions	Refrigerate	5 to 7 days	Do not wash until ready to use.	Remove band and store lightly wrapped in a dry paper towel in crisper drawer.
Snap peas	Refrigerate	3 to 5 days	Wash, trim, and steam to 2 minutes. Store in airtight glass for use in salads and wraps within 2 to 3 days of cooking. May also be eaten as a snack or frozen for future use.	Store in an open container draped with a damp towel in crisper drawer.
Spinach	Refrigerate	2 days	Do not wash until ready to use. Add to salads, juice, or blend into smoothies and soups.	Store loose in an open container in the crisper drawer. Do not store near melons, stone fruits, tomatoes, figs, bananas, or apples.
Sprouts	Refrigerate	1 to 2 days	Wash and dry thoroughly. Juice or add to salads.	Store uncovered in a shallow dish in main compartment of refrigerator. Do not store in crisper drawer.
Strawberries	Refrigerate	3 to 5 days	Do not wash until ready to use. Juice, blend, or add to salads and cereal. May wash and dry thoroughly and freeze immediately for future use.	Store unwashed in a paper bag in main compartment of refrigerator.
Summer squash	Room temperature	1 week	Wash and cut into disks for steaming, or grate atop salads.	Rest on countertop in a cool area. Do not store near melons, stone fruits, tomatoes, figs, bananas, or apples.
Sweet potatoes	Room temperature	2 months	Do not peel until ready to use.	Store in a cool, dark, dry, and well-ventilated place. Do not store near melons, stone fruits, tomatoes, figs, bananas, or apples.

FOOD	REFRIGERATE OR ROOM TEMPERATURE	DAYS TO REMAIN FRESH IF UNPREPPED	HOW TO PREP	HOW TO STORE IF NOT PREPPED
Swiss chard	Refrigerate	2 to 4 days	Do not wash until ready to use. Add to soups and stews or use for juicing.	Store unwashed and lightly packed in a fabric produce bag with a dry paper towel. Place in main compartment of refrigerator. Do not store near melons, stone fruits, tomatoes, figs, bananas, or apples.
Thyme	Refrigerate	5 days	Keep leaves attached to stems. Wash and dry thoroughly.	Store in container you bought it in or store in a loose, fabric produce bag with a dry paper towel inside to absorb excess moisture. Store in main compartment of refrigerator.
Tomatoes	Room temperature	5 to 7 days	Do not prep until ready to use.	Store on countertop in a well-ventilated area.
Watercress	Refrigerate	5 days	Do not wash until ready to use. Add to salads or juice the leaves.	Place just the stems in a glass of water and loosely drape the leaves with plastic. Remove wilting or discolored leaves. Do not store near melons, stone fruits, tomatoes, figs, bananas, or apples.
Winter squash	Room temperature	2 months	Peel, cube, and steam for 15 minutes. Store in airtight glass for use in soups, smoothies, pudding, or sauces, or as a snack. Enjoy within 3 to 5 days of cutting.	Store in a cool, dark, and well-ventilated place at room temperature. Do not store near melons, stone fruits, tomatoes, figs, bananas, or apples.
Zucchini	Room temperature	3 to 4 days	Wash and cut into disks for steaming, cube for soups, or cut into sticks for snacking.	Store on countertop in a well-ventilated area.

DON'T BE A JARHEAD

It is not unusual for the common household refrigerator to be overcome with jars of prepared salad dressings, sauces, marinades, and other condiments, but now that you are a Balanced Raw foodie, most of your condiments will be homemade and very few will be prepackaged. Those you do purchase should be organic and free of additives, sweeteners, and preservatives, and should be restocked every three to six months. You will learn in the next chapter how to look for harmful additives and preservatives found in most condiments, none of which are welcome in Balanced Raw living. These condiments are acceptable to buy rather than make from scratch: coconut aminos, organic Dijon mustard, capers, chickpea miso, white wine vinegar, apple cider vinegar (unfiltered with culture in the bottom), brown rice vinegar, mirin, balsamic vinegar, ume plum vinegar, raw tahini paste, raw almond butter, almond milk, raw maple syrup, hemp seed oil, cold-pressed and unfiltered olive oil, raw sauerkraut, sun-dried olives, and alcohol-free vanilla extract.

You will also want to store seeds in airtight, glass containers in your refrigerator to ensure freshness. Balanced Raw selections include chia seeds, sesame seeds (black and white), pumpkin seeds, sunflower seeds, and hemp seeds (hemp hearts).

GET YOUR GO-TO KITCHEN GADGETS

Behind every clean diet are a few key tools to simplify prep. You may be overwhelmed by the thousands of appealing kitchen gadgets touting bionic ability, but some are better, and more essential, than others and I share those with you here.

Straight edge peeler: Ceramic or stainless steel works well for peeling fruits and vegetables and creating vegetable ribbons.

VARY YOUR PRODUCE PREP TO MAKE IT POP

A great way to make fruits and vegetables more appealing and ready for use in a variety of dishes is to prep them in different ways.

For instance, cut half a bunch of carrots into sticks for snacking, and shred, julienne, or grate the other half for adding to wraps, salads, burgers, or other dishes. Radishes can be sliced or kept whole for snacking. Zucchini and summer squash can also be cut into sticks as well as cubed or cut into disks for steaming.

Prepping produce right when you get home increases your chances of using it up before it goes bad and reduces the amount of time you spend preparing your meals. You will also be less likely to reach for any garbage food if you have a well-stocked refrigerator full of prepped produce. Try to store cut fruits and vegetables in glass containers to ensure freshness. Stacked neatly, they allow you to quickly assess what you have on hand.

Some favorite snacking veggies are carrots, celery, cucumbers, zucchini, bell peppers, jicama, lightly steamed green beans, steamed asparagus, fresh kohlrabi, fennel, and celery root. Berries are also good to have on hand, as are apples, mango, figs, pears, kiwi, and pineapple.

Julienne peeler: Great if you do not have a mandoline (see below) for making very thin strips (matchsticks) of hard vegetables.

Vegetable/cheese grater: Ideal for finely grating vegetables such as beets, carrots, and zucchini if you do not have a food processor with a grater blade.

Vegetable steamer: This stainless steel basket fits in a variety of pots to make steaming vegetables and roots a breeze.

Salad spinner: Washing and drying lettuces are made simple with this handy device. Just throw washed leaves into the spinner, pull the lever or cord or turn the handle, and the greens spin their way to dryness. Also great for washing and drying fresh herbs.

High-quality chef's knife: This is the one tool that often gets purchased without it being high quality. It is imperative you outfit your kitchen with a professional knife that ergonomically fits your hand, and you feel comfortable using for chopping, mincing, slicing, and dicing. Selecting stainless steel or ceramic blades is left to personal preference. Try out a few until you find a match made in heaven. Never submerge your knife in water or put it in the dishwasher, and keep the blade dry as much as possible by wiping it frequently with a kitchen cloth during meal prep.

Citrus press: You will likely be hand-pressing limes and lemons for many dishes, and a citrus press will come in handy for separating the pulp and seeds from the juice. You do not need to purchase the lime press for limes, but rather just the lemon press to juice both.

Good-quality cutting board: Maple or bamboo boards are well liked. Get one large enough for cutting lots of vegetables at one time and avoid plastic cutting boards because these will dull your knives faster. Maintain the quality of your board by applying mineral oil once a month.

Vitamix or other high-speed blender: Although a bit of an investment, this is an absolute must for a Balanced Raw foodie, and many of the recipes in this book require the use of such an appliance. The suction power of these types of blenders continuously draws the food down to the blade in such an efficient way that the result is always smooth and silky sauces, dressings, puréed soups, and smoothies. You can also purchase dry containers for the Vitamix to grind your own flours and meals from grains, seeds, and nuts.

Juicer (highly recommended for included recipes): There are two types of juicers I recommend for doing the job efficiently, and selecting one always comes down to personal preference. The first of the two is a centrifugal juicer and the second is known as a masticating type. The centrifugal version is the most popular because of its speedy production time. When fruits and vegetables are pressed through the large-mouthed chute, a blade grinds them and passes them through a strainer at very high speed. The pulp is then deposited into an attached container at the back. Compared to a masticating juicer, the yield of juice is less and the pulp a bit more moist. Also, centrifugal juicers cannot juice wheatgrass.

A masticating juicer, sometimes referred to as a wheat-grass juicer, slowly chews through the fibers of fruits and vegetables, grinding at the cells to yield the highest quality and quantity of fresh juice. Masticating juicers can also be used to make ice cream, baby food, and seed butters. Their production time is much slower, but many people still like the versatility of this type. A tip for purchasing a juicer is to check community sites such as Craigslist for a used one. Often people buy a juicer with the best intentions to use it, only to sell it at reduced rate after only a few uses.

Food processor (optional but recommended): Having this powerful machine saves a ton of time on chopping a bunch of vegetables for a slaw, chopped salad, or when making treats, burgers, and baked goods.

Mortar and pestle: I almost always mash garlic into a paste using a mortar and pestle and love to make spice blends by crushing together whole peppercorns and other spices such as cumin and coriander seeds.

Mandoline (optional): This handy tool is useful for slicing and shaving vegetables and fruit into very thin strips or disks. Many also have julienne attachments for matchstick cuts. If you use a mandoline, always use the finger guard because the blade is extremely sharp.

Spice/coffee grinder (optional): This appliance is not required but is certainly handy for crushing nuts, dried herbs, and other spices.

THE SECOND LAYER OF YOUR FOUNDATION: CULTIVATE AN ATTITUDE OF GRATITUDE AND LEARN TO EXPRESS YOURSELF

Every time you embark on a journey into cleansing, detoxing, or redefining your relationship with food, you are likely to experience physical and emotional side effects. Sometimes these effects are mild and other times more intense, but in either case, these responses to bodily changes are completely normal and acceptable.

As you shed unhealthy lifestyle habits and addictions, your body and mind may purge negative thought patterns, beliefs that no longer serve you, fears, and even debilitating compulsions. This transformation period is as much about psychological realignment as it is physical. Do not be alarmed, as with all transformation comes an uncomfortable or enlightening period. To ease discomfort, reflect often on your intentions, and try to cultivate an attitude of gratitude.

An exercise that is sure to support a positive and gracious attitude is to make a list every morning of all you are grateful for. Combine this activity with a breathing technique you can use any time to quiet your mind and turn your attention inward for self-reflection and calm. To complete this simple morning exercise, follow these ten steps:

1. At bedtime, set your alarm to wake you at least ten minutes earlier so you will have time to complete this activity without haste and with full expression.

2. When you awake, give your entire body a good stretch.

3. Make your favorite morning beverage, whether juice, tea, or warm water with lemon.

4. Grab your drink, journal, and a pen, and find a comfortable place to sit in the most peaceful room in your house.

5. Close your eyes and turn your attention to your breathing. Take five deep inhales and five deep exhales, ensuring each is at least three seconds long.

6. Hold your breath between inhales and exhales long enough to focus on the sound of your beating heart.

7. As you breathe, imagine visiting the most peaceful place your mind can visualize. Maybe you see the beach, the forest, or a beautiful garden, or maybe you at the peak of a majestic mountain.

8. As you actualize this image and visualize yourself there, take five more inhales and exhales and feel your presence in the picture of your mind. Express gratitude for experiencing such a calm state.

9. Then gently open your eyes and write down all you are grateful for and include anything big or small—from your ability to see and hear, freedom to choose, your access to clean food and water, your gifts and talents, or any person, trait, or comfort you are blessed with.

10. Seal this exercise by setting an intention for the day. Maybe it is to live more in the present moment, greet everyone with a smile, do something kind for someone else unsolicited, or act with care toward those you share your home with. Whatever it is, hold it in your mind, go about getting ready for your day, and return to the breathing steps whenever you feel discouraged, restless, or distracted.

With all of life's challenges, you have two choices in how to deal with them. You can either let them get you down, become discouraged, depressed, sad, or frustrated, or even give up. The other way to respond is with the spirit of gratitude. This means you accept the challenge with grace. You welcome the challenge with the confidence that it will make you stronger, teach you a valuable lesson, introduce you to a new world, people, cultures, or way of thinking, or accept that it may enhance your gifts and talents.

This is one of those times to act with grace and gratitude. As you journey into transformation, welcome the change. Accept the mild or intense discomfort you may feel as temporary. Tender self-care and a positive outlook will help you accept this transformation, knowing it is only temporary and that the payoff is you achieving a nourished, whole, and balanced body with all of its systems working in harmony and achievement of the physical, mental, or spiritual goals you have set for yourself.

You can experience deep relief through writing in a journal and later revisiting your words of encouragement, wisdom, and wonder. As you move through the four phases of the Balanced Raw system, thoughts and emotions may surface and writing them down gets them out in front of you for reflection and consideration.

If you do not already have an adored journal, go to your favorite bookstore or retail outlet and pick one up that speaks to you. Keep your bound buddy with you at all times and take note of those emotional pieces of you that rise to the surface.

Be sure to write down any biological changes as well. Maybe your skin begins to clear or your eyes brighten. Perhaps your allergies subside or you begin to enjoy more restful sleep. Track your physical progress to the degree of detail most comfortable for you.

As you detox, it is not unusual to have feelings of sadness, anxiety, guilt, or anger. Jot down these negative emotions to keep them from building up inside you. I will say again, this is as much a psychological transformation as it is physical! Write every day, even if it is just a few simple thoughts like, "I feel tired," "I have lost two pounds," or "The Ruby Rabbit Pressed Juice is really good!" A written statement, big or small, will help carry you through to total transformation.

Remember that your body shows up for you every single day without force. All on its own, it breathes, sees, smells, walks, runs, and functions without you telling it to. It serves you day after day with unconditional love. Your body never complains unless abused and does all it can to give you a good life. Consider these next four weeks and beyond as a time to give back to your body. If you have been hurting it with processed food, chemicals, artificial sweeteners, or excess fat, or if you have robbed it of balanced nutrients, restful sleep, or exercise, this is the time to honor its hard work and give it the nurturing and care it deserves.

THE THIRD LAYER OF YOUR FOUNDATION: ALLOW YOUR BODY TIME TO ADJUST TO OPTIMUM HEALTH AND VITALITY

Have you ever watched a snake shed its scaling skin, or a locust emerge from its translucent shell? Imagine the discomfort they both must experience as they shed the old, crusty, and colorless facade to reveal a more vibrant and youthful species. They must experience some aches and pains and perhaps become a bit exhausted.

During the elimination, cleansing, and restoration phases, you, too, may experience symptoms of shedding the old as you dissolve destructive habits and expel built-up toxins. Your body will be introduced to an existence free of preservatives and additives, artificial sweeteners, and processed foods. As it is restricted from consuming food allergens and sensitivity-promoting foods, it is provided the opportunity to call on its energy reserves to bring new and clean blood and nutrients to all organs and awaken them from a dormant state.

TOXINS MAY CAUSE TWISTED SLEEP

If your body is very toxic, you may experience bizarre or negative dreams or even nightmares during the detoxing period. This, too, is a normal response to cleansing, but it can be disturbing. Keep your journal and a pen by your bedside and if you wake from such a dream or nightmare, write down your emotions immediately to free the uncomfortable thoughts. Practice the breathing exercise outlined earlier in the chapter to help ease you back to sleep.

When you stop feeding your body processed foods filled with additives and chemicals, your heart, brain, kidneys, lungs, liver, and pancreas all begin to work more efficiently. When this happens, toxic buildup is finally able to be expelled from your skin, mouth, bowels, and mucous membranes. Pimples, rashes, and other breakouts may occur but are temporary. This is a healthy sign you are letting the nasty buggers out! You will likely experience some changes in bowel movements; perhaps you will have looser stools or alterations in their color. Do note, however, excessive diarrhea is not a good sign, and if you experience this you should consult your physician. Your sinuses may either clear, which often happens when someone suffers from seasonal allergies, or they may get worse for a time as your body purges the toxins.

It is possible to experience fatigue and muscle and joint aches or weakness as your energy is being allocated to organ function. Embrace this time and know that you are replacing these expelled toxins with fresh, oxygenated, and nutrient-rich blood, sending it to vital organs, allowing them to heal and repair. To reduce discomfort and to clear your mind, give your body plenty of rest and participate in mellow activities such as walking, yoga, and stretching. If you are fatigued and if your schedule allows, take a midday nap. If you have a demanding job that requires acute focus and you cannot risk being tired, bring an extra energizing smoothie or pressed juice such as the Ruby Rabbit (see page 113) with you to the office. Alternatively, sip on anti-oxidant-rich green or yerba maté teas.

DE-CLUTTER YOUR CALENDAR WHILE CLEARING THE TOXINS

Truly there never seems to be a right time for cleansing. You could make social events a reason to put it off along with luncheons, birthdays, and corporate parties, but unless you make your cleansing period a priority and clear social clutter, you may never get around to this critical period for renewed health. Your commitment to this transformation requires only one week of a simplified schedule, and the payoff is worth ignoring every whim to be out and about.

If at all possible, begin your cleanse at the very start of a weekend so that for a couple of days you are easing into the effects of a lighter diet and can fully experience the transformative effects of purging toxins. It is helpful to notify others of your week's plan, and in the process you may even recruit a cleansing companion simply from speaking up. Having a buddy always helps to keep you on track. With or without a buddy, make sure you can be home, or near home for at least the first two or three days to make your meals, relax, and give your body the opportunity to restore and rejuvenate. Beyond the initial cleansing period, returning to work is appropriate; just try to avoid happy hours and other night outings and instead come right home to work on you. Alternatively, spend your evenings at a yoga class or go for a walk or run. Many yoga studios offer a free week if you haven't been before, and this would be a great opportunity to practice your downward dog.

As with all of life's changes, there are periods of discomfort, adaptability, and transformation, and adoption of the Balanced Raw lifestyle is no different. Just know the results are profoundly positive and the suggestions made in this chapter will help reduce the side effects that may arise. Are you ready? It is time to go to work on discovering the new you!

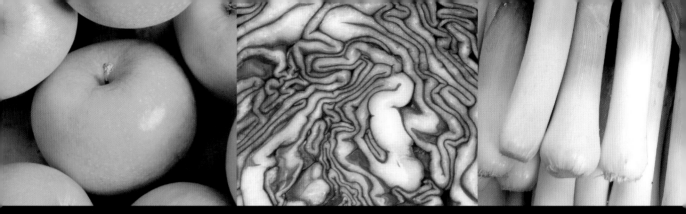

{ Part 2 }

THE
BALANCED RAW
SYSTEM

CHAPTER 4

WEEK 1 ELIMINATE

REMOVE ALLERGY-PROMOTING AND ACID-FORMING FOODS

ELIMINATION-FRIENDLY RECIPES

- Red Cabbage, Asparagus, and Radish Slaw with Mustard Vinaigrette

- Cauliflower Rice Collard Wrap with Crunchy Vegetables and Lemon-Tahini Sauce

- Raw Zucchini Noodles with Fresh Tomatoes, Sun-Dried Olives, and Kale Pesto

- Big Herb Salad with Creamy Garlic and Spirulina Dressing

- Pumpkin Spice Morning Chia Porridge

- Blue Greens Smoothie

- Veggie Blast Fresh Pressed Juice

- Celery Root and Leek Soup with Green Apple

- Glowing Greens and Hemp Soup

- Spirulina Coconut Truffles

- Chili-Lime Veggie Crudité

- Shaved Roots and Herbed Parsnip Stack

- Carrot Noodles with Bean Sprouts, Cabbage, and Miso-Ginger Sauce

- Tamarind Tossed Squash Noodles

- Hidden Greens Chocolate Shake

YOU HAVE READ THIS FAR, SO I KNOW YOU ARE COMMITTED to elevating your well-being and ready to take the steps necessary to achieve a sustainable, Balanced Raw lifestyle. Completing the elimination phase will deepen your commitment and prepare your body and mind for gentle detoxification and restoration. This phase is essential in building a solid foundation for healthy living. During the next seven days, you will reshape your eating environment and relationship with food. This phase is where healthy habits are made. Are you ready? Let's get started.

Eliminating garbage food from your eating environment is essential in developing healthy habits and requires only four simple steps and a day of devotion.

STEP 1: EVALUATE AND EXTRACT

Begin the first step by evaluating the condition of your eating environment. Stop and take a look at the foods stored in your kitchen. Are your shelves stocked with expired foods? Are any older than six months? Older than a year?

How about processed foods, such as chemical-ridden snacks, cereals, and condiments with outrageous levels of refined sugars, or chips and crackers rich in hydrogenated oils and artificial flavoring? Do you have any of these body-harming foods in your cupboards?

If your shelves are stocked with instant oatmeal, prepared soups, microwavable popcorn (or anything microwavable for that matter), or canned or jarred spaghetti sauce, you have garbage food. Do your best to eliminate all canned, jarred, and packaged foods where the nutrition labels include ingredients beyond the main food, water, and salt. If you have a can of chickpeas and the only other ingredients are water and salt, there is no need to eliminate it. Just remember, you will want to use fresh and dried ingredients whenever possible and reserve canned goods for a time crunch. Remove all junk from your shelves, and line them up like valiant soldiers on your kitchen counter. You will be sizing them up shortly.

STEP 2: ADD SOME ELBOW GREASE EACH MONTH

Many of the supportive foods you will be stocking are those purchased in bulk and without packaging, and it is important that cupboard and pantry surfaces be clean and sanitary to avoid the infestation of pests and growth of bacteria. Give your kitchen a fresh finish by wiping all surfaces with a nontoxic cleansing agent. Get down and dirty, and scrub the grease, dust, and grime from your shelves and countertops. Your mission is to have a shiny clean slate to stock with nutritious, Balanced Raw–friendly foods.

To avoid future invasions of pests and the accumulation of mold, commit to thoroughly scrubbing your kitchen surfaces at least once per month. With all the fresh herbs and greens you will be stocking, your refrigerator will likely have remnants of such, and it is a good idea to wipe it out each time you restock, as well as monthly.

STEP 3: REVIEW AND DISCARD

Your next step is to review the nutrition labels of all foods displayed on your countertop. Check expiration dates and throw out those foods that have expired.

Look for preservatives that fall into a trash bin I like to call "adverse additives." These include any chemical or food toxins. Though studies may disagree on the level of their toxicity, some countries have banned these addivites, and a great deal of research suggests they promote cellular damage, reduce your immunity, and thus promote chronic and inflammatory diseases such as diabetes, arthritis, cancer, heart disease, hypertension, candida, colds, and flu.

There are more than three thousand additives in our processed food supply today that have been approved by the U.S. Food and Drug Administration (FDA) as safe for human consumption, yet numerous studies link them to various diseases and disorders. To address all three thousand additives is outside the scope of this book, but the most common are listed on the chart on page 50.

I am sure you will agree this information is disturbing, and what is even more frightening is the FDA does not require color additives to be naturally derived. As a matter of fact, the FDA discourages the use of natural pigments, such as grape skins, beets, annatto, and beta-carotene, as these nonsynthetic sources are more expensive, may result in color inconsistency, and may alter the flavor profile of the food. Before food dyes were manufactured like they are today, people used natural fruit and spice pigments, such as beets, for coloring red velvet cakes and Easter eggs. I would much rather pay a few extra cents and risk color variance to have a natural food product. Wouldn't you?

THROW OUT THE JUNK AND WELCOME HEALTH INTO YOUR HOME AND BODY

So now that you have received a lesson in garbage food, let's revisit your kitchen counter lined with the processed foods you pulled. If you have nuts and oils that have been hanging around for three months or more, or oils that have been exposed to sunlight or heat, or if you have oil-containing processed foods, they need to be discarded. You will never really know how long chips have occupied a bag before making their way to grocery shelves and then into your home. I guarantee it has been too long.

ADDITIVE	PURPOSE	HEALTH IMPLICATIONS
Sodium benzoate	Extends shelf life	ADHD, migraines, and cancer
Nitrates and nitrites	Microorganism growth inhibitors	Alzheimer's, heart disease, Parkinson's, and type 2 diabetes
Butylated hydroxyanisole (BHA)	Prevents fat rancidity	Cancer
Diglycerides	Emulsifiers	Heart disease and type 2 diabetes
Potassium bromate	Increases volume in baked goods	Cancer
Aspartame	Chemical sweetener	Multiple sclerosis, Parkinson's, and fibromyalgia
Hydrogenated oils	Extends shelf life	Heart disease and type 2 diabetes
High-fructose corn syrup (HFCS)	Processed sweetening agent	Liver disease, type 2 diabetes, obesity, and ADHD
Monosodium and potassium glutamates	Flavor enhancement	Alzheimer's, type 2 diabetes, and obesity
Synthetic colors including Blue No. 1, Red No. 3, Red No. 40, Yellow No. 5, and Caramel Color	Food pigment and hue enhancement	Cancer and ADHD

If, on the nutrition labels of your foods, you see *sugar, corn sweetener, corn syrup solids, high-fructose corn syrup (HFCS)*, any one of the additives listed above, or words that are difficult to pronounce, like *butylated hydroxytoluene,* an additive used to keep food from spoiling, you will want to rid your home and body of them and toss them out. Discard them with glee and pat yourself on the back for taking a huge step toward sustained health and vitality.

When I was a child, my mom had jars of dried rice, whole-wheat flour, oats, and barley, and they were stacked high in our pantry nestled between Chex Mix, Kix cereal, and Pringles potato chips. I will never forget one Sunday morning when Mom pulled the flour and oats out for us to bake with and the flour was infested with weevils. We were so disgusted by their presence and terrified there might be more that we went tearing through all other jars of grains as well as every packaged food item to ensure there weren't more insects hiding in our food. We did discover others, but only in the jars of barley and rice. There was no sign of them in the chips, cereal, or crackers. Even at that very young age, I thought, "That's so weird, they only want the natural foods." Looking back, it is no surprise that even insects do not find food with monosodium glutamate or HFCS appetizing. When given the option, weevils will select all-natural foods as they recognize the processed selections as devoid of nutrients.

AVOID ADVERSE ADDITIVES AND AID YOUR LIVER

Behind the facade of food packaging is an army of chemicals and toxins, and the nasty effects of these additives come as a result of the liver not being able to process such unnatural ingredients and toxins. This vital organ is responsible for nearly five hundred functions and, most importantly, detoxification. Once toxins are consumed, the liver is supposed to pass them on to your large intestine, where they are prepped for elimination.

However, when you consume toxins in excess, some of them do not get passed on. They build up and the liver is then tasked with passing them while tending to its other responsibilities, which becomes a burden. When this happens, less detoxification occurs and the liver stores these chemicals. The liver can only hold so many and is forced to release these poisons into the bloodstream, which is the delivery system to all other organs. When your organs are attacked, all bodily functions are in danger and you can begin to experience digestive distress, fatigue, obesity, and possibly even diabetes, heart and brain disease, and cancer.

So as you can see, all your organs take a beating when you regularly consume additives and preservatives. The Balanced Raw system is about developing a lifestyle of balanced and healthy eating habits to keep these organs happy and healthy.

So if the foods you pulled from your refrigerator and cupboards contain any food toxin in the form of preservatives, colorings, or additives, set them aside for discharge. They are no longer fit for your home or body.

BREAK FROM FREE RADICALS FOR HEALTHY CELLS AND DISEASE RESISTANCE

Consuming chemicals and additives opens the door for them not only to harm your organs but also to promote the production of free radicals. Free radicals are atoms that have an odd number of electrons, and having unpaired electrons makes them unstable. One of the highest priorities of atoms is to remain stable by having a complete outer shell of electron pairs. Free radicals spend their time traveling from one atom to the next, trying to gain the attention of other electrons in order to create bonds, become grounded, and thus gain stability. Out of desperation they will go to great lengths to banish instability, even by robbing a stable molecule of its electrons.

This action causes a domino effect of instability in atoms and results in degeneration of your cells. This domino effect speeds the aging process, reduces the strength of your immune system, promotes illness, and disrupts the harmony of your body's functions and systems. Free radicals are so miserable alone that if given permission to enter your body by way of chemical-ridden foods, they will rob you of your youthfulness and vitality.

Free radicals are so miserable alone that if given permission to enter your body by way of chemical-ridden foods, they will rob you of your youthfulness and vitality.

Beware of Free Radicals in Nuts and Oils

One common place to note the production of free radicals is in polyunsaturated fats, such as canola, safflower, sunflower, soybean, and corn oils, as well as prepared foods containing these oils, including salad dressings, dips, spreads, condiments, crackers, cookies, and chips. Unlike saturated fats, those that are polyunsaturated lack pairs of atoms. A lack of strong atomic bond promotes instability as they try to steal hydrogen atoms from the air. This action is known as oxidation and happens whenever unsaturated fats are exposed to air, light, or heat. The result is degradation and breakdown of the product, referred to as rancidity. When consumed, this oxidative reaction creates an imbalance at the cellular level, and this imbalance greatly disrupts the health of your body.

Sesame and olive oils contain a higher percentage of monounsaturated fats, which are missing only one pair of hydrogen atoms, making them a bit more stable, yet still vulnerable when heated and exposed to light. If you choose to use olive and sesame oils, refrigerate them in dark glass bottles, and reserve for use in uncooked foods such as homemade dressings and pestos, and for drizzling on salads and other dishes. Do not use them for cooking and restock frequently, about every two to three months, to ensure freshness.

The only oil suitable for cooking and heating is coconut oil because it is almost an entirely saturated fat, containing multiple hydrogen atom pairs, making it extremely stable when heated or exposed to light.

You also find monounsaturated and polyunsaturated fats in nuts such as macadamia, pine, cashew, Brazil, almond, pistachio, peanut, hazel, and walnut, and to ensure they are not prone to rancidity, buy often and refrigerate.

Eating oil-containing processed foods such as those mentioned earlier, as well as nuts and oils that have not been refrigerated, those that are older than three months, or those that have been heated, welcomes free radicals to enter your cells, and as you now know accelerates aging and promotes disease. Remove them from your eating environment and restock with a fresh batch.

Also, as you learned in chapter 2, you will want to limit your use of coconut, or any oil, to a drizzle, and to no more than 10 percent of your daily caloric intake. If you consume 2,000 calories per day, 10 percent would equate to only 200 fat calories, or roughly three-fourths of a medium avocado, 2 to 3 tablespoons (28 to 42 g) of seeds, or 2 tablespoons (28 ml) of oil. These amounts are for the entire day, so select your fats wisely and use those that are most satisfying.

Seeds are well liked because of their crunch, as are avocados because of their buttery flavor and smooth and creamy texture.

ELIMINATE ADDICTIVE SUGARS FOR WEIGHT LOSS, INCREASED METABOLISM, AND A HEALTHY LIVER

More disease-promoting glops of garbage are refined sugar, sweeteners, and high-fructose corn syrup, a concentrated liquid sweetener. All are found in nearly every packaged food from hamburger buns to salad dressings, canned soups, and crackers. You have likely heard from friends and family to avoid refined sugar and HFCS, but do you know why? Let me enlighten you.

Their chemical structure encourages an addictive response by elevating levels of serotonin, a neurotransmitter responsible for reducing anxiety and depression, and increasing feelings of happiness and well-being. In addition, sugar also activates the release of dopamine, the same endorphin released during drug use and linked to feelings of reward. When you begin eating processed sugars, the time lapse between each consumption produces only a mild desire to eat it again, yet over time, the urges become stronger and you consume more to combat feelings of withdrawal.

Eating sugar and then going without it makes you overeat in order to satisfy your cravings and maintain feelings of pleasure.

Your body was not designed to assimilate such concentrated and excess levels of fructose. Unless sugars are burned quickly, like when they're consumed right before a workout, the excess carbohydrates are converted to, and stored as, fat. Also, studies show refined sugars and HFCS disrupt metabolism, leading to diabetes and heart disease, task the liver by producing elevated levels of triglycerides, and promote insulin resistance. Those results sound pretty awful to me.

The sad reality is that refined sugar and HFCS are found in almost every available packaged food. Did you know there is the exact amount of sugar (5 teaspoons, or 20 g) in a serving of store-bought tomato sauce as there is in chocolate syrup? Why on earth would tomato sauce have as much sugar as a dessert enhancement? Food manufacturers add sugar to reduce the acidic flavor profile of tomatoes, which is silly, because that is how they are supposed to taste and they sweeten naturally when cooked down. Also, as I mentioned previously, because sugar and HFCS encourage an addictive response, you must eat beyond the recommended serving size to feel satisfied.

Because sugar and high-fructose corn syrup encourage an addictive response, you must eat beyond the recommended serving size to feel satisfied.

The sugar added to tomato sauce is just one example of the unnecessary ingredients being added to packaged foods to make you crave, eat, and buy more. Be informed and read your labels carefully. Disregard the bold statements on the front of the package claiming the product is made from "whole grains," with "natural sweeteners," or is "low in fat." These marketing tactics are used to lure you in and make you buy. If you turn over the package and scrutinize the list of ingredients, you will see the loads of junk that, starting now, you will want to avoid introducing into the one and only body you have.

CURB CAFFEINE FOR MOOD REGULATION, FOCUS, AND ENERGY

When you are suddenly met with danger, your heart pumps wildly, your palms sweat, and your breathing shallows. Your body enters a state of emergency. These are the same effects caffeine has on your system. These fight-or-flight sensations may not be noticeable to you; however, they are happening. Your seemingly innocent cup of joe puts your body on a roller-coaster ride most would fear and disrupts your mood, energy, and concentration, which is likely the opposite of what you think it does.

Most caffeine users rely on the drug for acute focus, increased stamina and energy, and elevation of mood. So why would I say that it has the opposite effect? Because although caffeine does stimulate your nerve centers to give you that anticipated jolt of energy and makes you feel alert and happy, these results are short lived and within only a few uses of caffeine, your body requires much more of the drug more times throughout the day to achieve the same sensations. The ups, downs, twists, and turns of caffeine use burden your body with unseen stress throughout the day and even into twilight hours.

Immediately as you ingest caffeine, whether from coffee, black or green tea, soda, energy drinks, or in supplement form, the drug stimulates your central nervous system (CNS) and releases the stress hormones *epinephrine* (adrenaline) and *norepinephrine*, thrusting your body into fight-or-flight mode. This is the state you are in when met with danger. Routinely alerting your CNS this way results in some very disturbing bodily responses such as adrenal burnout and disrupted cortisol levels. Both sound pretty ominous, don't they? They are.

After the enchanting effects of your initial caffeine high wear off, you crash. A mildly notable crash to you, however, feels like a cataclysmic crash to your nervous system. So what do you do? You reach for more caffeine or even sugar during the slump to stimulate you again. The constant secretion of stress hormones from the adrenal glands causes what's known as adrenal burnout, sometimes called adrenal fatigue or exhaustion.

Adrenal fatigue can lead to insomnia because it causes the levels of cortisol (the hormone that regulates sleep and energy) to rise and fall at the wrong times of the day. Cortisol production should mimic the natural cycles of day and night, rising in the morning hours, and then tapering off in the evening to help you sleep. The tossing and turning and unrestful sleep you may be familiar with is often due to surges in cortisol at bedtime.

The bottom line is caffeine does not provide energy, but rather the illusion of energy. Caffeine is an addictive drug and you are better off without it. This is not to say that enjoying a tasty cup of organic coffee, matcha (a celebratory Japanese green tea), or antioxidant-rich yerba maté from time to time will leave you depleted and out of whack, but making a routine habit of consuming caffeinated beverages is detrimental to your health.

You won't need caffeine if you are eating nourishing foods; making time to meditate, breathe, and rest; going to sleep and rising at nearly the same time every day and getting at least seven hours of sleep per night; regularly exercising; and living in a state of peace rather than chaos.

Just a word of caution as you kick the caffeine habit. If you do so cold turkey, you may experience withdrawal symptoms such as depression, anxiety, irritability, confusion, lack of focus, nervousness, fatigue, headaches, and disrupted sleep. These withdrawal symptoms are temporary and usually do not last more than seven days after putting down the drug. Reduce these uncomfortable side effects with rest, by enjoying complex carbohydrates such as starchy vegetables, grains, and beans, and including naturally stimulating herbs such as ginseng and maca root to your supplement routine. If you are having trouble sleeping, try sipping a bit of chamomile tea before bed or take herbs such as ashwagandha, schizandra, valerian root, or vetiver.

STEP 4: ORGANIZE AND RESTOCK YOUR SHELVES

Now that your army of processed foods has been properly discharged, you will want to organize and restock your pantry and refrigerator only with healthy foods. A devoted Balanced Raw foodie will not have one half of his or her pantry filled with junk and the other stocked with natural foods.

Even though you will be avoiding certain healthful and Balanced Raw–supporting foods during this and the next phase, this is the time to stock up so you are prepared for weeks 3, 4, and beyond. Remember, the elimination phase is about building the foundation. Use this time to shop for the bulk grains, whole-grain flour, spices, seeds, and legumes listed and described in chapter 3.

Remember, you will want to store ingredients in glass, so if you do not already have proper storage containers, you can find inexpensive glass jars at thrift stores, or buy a couple of cases of mason jars, and voilà! You have dry good storage. Glass keeps food safe from toxins potentially

The bottom line is caffeine does not provide energy, but rather the illusion of energy.

present in plastics, and glass is nonporous, keeping it free from absorbing food particles and germs. Glass can also be washed and sanitized at high temperatures, unlike plastic, and storing food in glass helps maintain the integrity of the food because it keeps odors from penetrating and altering the flavor profile.

REDUCE ACID-, ALLERGY-, AND SENSITIVITY-PROMOTING FOODS

As part of the elimination phase, you will be avoiding the consumption of those foods most commonly associated with allergies and sensitivities, such as corn, soy, gluten, dairy, and nuts.

Food allergens cause immune reactions of multiple organs and can be severe and even life-threatening, such as in the case of anaphylaxis. Food sensitivities are not as serious and are limited to digestive responses such as gas, bloating, constipation, or diarrhea. A food allergen will likely cause a digestive response accompanied by other immune system flares such as hives, headaches, vomiting, tingling or swelling of the face, throat, and tongue, and wheezing or shortness of breath. A food allergen will likely produce symptoms if even a single particle of the allergen is consumed. In the case of sensitivity, a food can often be eaten with very mild reactions and the symptoms can generally be reduced with digestive aids and enzymes.

One simple test to see whether you have a food sensitivity is to eliminate that food for a time and then reintroduce it and monitor your body's response, which you will do in week 3, the restore phase. To determine whether you suffer from a true food allergy, a blood test can be administered by your health care practitioner.

You may not be aware of symptoms of sensitivity or allergies to soy, corn, gluten, dairy, or nuts, but they could silently be reducing your immunity, causing digestive distress, fatigue, lack of sleep, and congestion, or contributing to head or body aches. Eliminating these common allergens for these next couple of weeks will provide your body the opportunity to restore its natural healing processes and set you up for success in your Balanced Raw lifestyle.

There are five common food allergens and below you will find a description of each, general symptoms that result from an allergy or a sensitivity, and suggestions for eliminating them from your diet.

Corn. Corn is a less-common yet known allergen, with sometimes very severe reactions. In addition, 93 percent of corn products are cultivated using genetically modified organisms (GMOs), which means its genetic characteristics have been altered by the introduction of modified genes (or organisms) to produce higher product yields, ward off pests, or produce a higher content of nutrients.

Some studies show that when digested, genetically modified foods disrupt the harmony of healthy bacteria in the intestines. In late 2011, a study conducted by the Italian National Institute of Research for Food and Nutrition demonstrated that genetically modified corn caused mice to experience a negative immune response of inflammation because of the corn containing a gene known as "Bt," which produces a toxic pesticide. There are a number of studies like this that affirm genetic engineering is an unnatural process, promotes allergies, and suppresses the immune system. So unless it is non-GMO, corn is unwelcome in the Balanced Raw diet.

Earlier in this phase, you may have cleansed your kitchen of corn-containing foods just by discarding all processed junk, but in case there are some stragglers, you will want to check for and discard GMO maize, masa, popcorn, grits, hominy, polenta, and any products containing corn syrup, corn oil, meal, and starch, vegetable oil, margarine, corn tortilla chips, most salad dressings, baking mixes, ketchup, GMO corn tortillas, breakfast cereals, or any packaged foods containing dextrose, cerelose, sweetose, or glucose.

Soy. Soy allergies are common in children and increasingly so in adults. Known symptoms include nasal congestion, gastrointestinal disturbance, itching, acne, hives, and asthma. If you are confused by conflicting messages regarding the healthfulness of soy, you are not alone. Much of your confusion can be attributed to it appearing to be a staple food enjoyed throughout Asia. Soy, for decades, has also been touted as a nutritious baby formula and a healthful and sufficient vegetarian and vegan protein alternative.

One issue with soy is it contains phytoestrogens. Studies show these plant-based estrogens, when eaten in excess, may stimulate the growth of breast cancer cells and reduce testosterone levels in males, neither of which makes it sound worth eating.

Soy is also another common GMO product and should be eliminated to avoid the health complications associated with consumption of genetically modified foods.

Small quantities of soy products are acceptable in the Balanced Raw diet as long as they are derived from quality, non-GMO soy products such as those consumed in Asian cuisine, which do not include soy protein powder, tofu, or soy milk. These more common soy foods should be omitted during the elimination phase and eaten very rarely, if at all, in your ongoing Balanced Raw lifestyle.

Quality soy products include fermented Asian condiments such as natto, tempeh, nama shoyu, tamari, and miso. These nutrient- and probiotic-rich soy foods are enjoyed in Asian cuisine as an enhancement to a dish rather than eaten in abundance, as we frequently see with tofu and soy milk.

Fermentation predigests the soy and breaks down the proteins, making it easier to assimilate, and also reduces the presence of phytoestrogens as well as harmful phytic acid, which is responsible for creating barriers to mineral absorption.

Since you'll be avoiding all soy foods for the next two weeks, try a healthful soy sauce alternative derived from the coconut tree. Most health food stores now sell this product labeled coconut aminos. This salty condiment is sap extracted from the coconut tree and is rich in seventeen essential amino acids, is significantly lower in sodium, and has a near neutral pH.

Gluten. Because the brain and gastrointestinal system are so closely connected, a disruption in one can cause the other to be affected. You see this in the case of nervousness or anxiety. When you are nervous, you may experience "butterflies" in your stomach. When you are anxious, your stomach may feel queasy or your appetite may be supressed. You see the results of this gut-mind connection in the case of some food sensitivities, such as gluten. The most common symptoms of gluten sensitivity are depression, brain fog, fatigue, and unexplained weight gain. The neurological effects occur because gluten is causing an imbalance in the gut, which in turn affects the health of your brain.

Gluten is a protein found in rye, wheat, wheat bran, barley, and triticale, and it is responsible for adding chewiness, elasticity, density, and structure to pastas, baked goods, packaged foods, and desserts, among other foods. It also helps retain the gases created during the fermentation of dough, thus allowing bread to rise before it is baked. Essentially, it makes breads, sweets, crackers, and cereals more tasty and appealing.

Please note gluten sensitivity is different from celiac disease, an autoimmune disease in which sufferers absolutely cannot consume gluten because it damages their small intestines. Perhaps you do not have any of the listed symptoms but have been inundated with advertisements, commentary, labels, and coffee talk all boasting the benefits of gluten avoidance. Whether you are curious about the statement "gluten-free is the way to be," or think gluten may be responsible for general malaise or fatigue you may be feeling, read on.

Remember the need to throw out anything processed? One reason is most of it has gluten. Too much gluten. Gluten has always been present in our food supply, but to make food more appetizing, excessive amounts of gluten are added. Our bodies are not able to break down such high amounts of the protein, and so we see gluten intolerance and sensitivity.

Now onto celiac disease. About 1 percent of the American population has celiac disease, and the condition is very serious. People afflicted are entirely unable to digest gluten, and their systems are grossly disrupted when even a trace of the protein enters the body. They must avoid foods such as oats and teff, which are not naturally gluten-containing foods but could have been cross-contaminated if grown or processed near gluten-containing foods.

Someone with celiac disease also must avoid most body and skin care products, including shampoo, body wash, cosmetics, lip balm, and even toothpaste, as they almost always contain gluten. Whether you have a noticeable gluten intolerance, sensitivity, or celiac disease, your body will thank you for opting to consume whole, gluten-free grains and unprocessed foods.

Dairy. Does dairy still have a place in your diet? If so, you may find the following information quite alarming. In a comprehensive twenty-year study, known as the China Study, researchers demonstrated how casein, the main protein in cow's milk, promotes a cancer-thriving environment. The reduction or increase of casein when presented in conjunction with an already toxin-exposed organism (which we all are) will literally turn off and turn on the growth of cancer cells, according to the study.

Author T. Colin Campbell, Ph.D., says in his book, *The China Study*, which is a compilation of the project's results and analysis, that thousands of studies were conducted to demonstrate that when rats consumed a diet with 5 percent casein, cancer cell growth turned off. When given 20 percent casein, cancer growth turned on again.

Dairy is also very acidic to the system and in a moment you will learn about why you want a more alkaline pH balance. So show your body some love, and just give up the dairy.

Nuts. If you are nuts about nuts, eating them regularly throughout the day, it is possible this overabundance is not serving your body in the highest and best way possible. As you learned in chapter 2, nuts contain unhealthy levels of omega-6 fatty acids, and too many omega-6s promote inflammation. You also now know they contain high levels of monounsaturated and polyunsaturated fats, making them unstable if not refrigerated and restocked frequently.

Peanuts, cashews, hazelnuts, Brazil nuts, pecans, pistachios, macadamia nuts, and walnuts have an allergy-promoting property that affects an estimated 1.8 million Americans. The property is their protein. Many people experience allergic reactions when they consume nuts; their body believes the protein is a nasty invader and reacts by creating antibodies. These antibodies release histamines, chemicals that attack the protein, and this can affect multiple systems of the body just like you saw in the case of soy, corn, and gluten. Symptoms may include disruptions in gastrointestinal health, hives and rashes, vomiting, wheezing, and shortness of breath.

In some, the allergic response is anaphylaxis, a sometimes deadly response with symptoms that include heart palpitations, skin redness, slurred speech, wheezing, and difficulty breathing from restricted airways. In others, an allergic response to nuts may go unnoticed on the surface, but it could be wreaking havoc on digestive health and immunity. Some symptoms associated with milder nut allergies include skin rashes, gas, bloating, constipation, diarrhea, headaches, joint pain, fatigue, and sinus congestion. See how you feel after eliminating these potential allergens for the next two weeks. Once reintroduced, you may continue to enjoy nuts, but do so in moderation and be sure to refrigerate nuts in glass containers to keep them from going rancid.

During this elimination week, take notes in your journal of how you feel each day. Jot down whether you feel energized, have a reduction in joint pain or headaches, or notice morning congestion subsiding or acid reflux diminishing. You will review your notes in chapter 7 to see at which points you felt your best, and as you reintroduce some allergen-associated foods back into your diet, one at a time, those notes will provide value for you to compare how you feel then to when you first started.

EAT AN ABUNDANCE OF NUTRIENT-RICH VEGETABLES

During this first week, you will be readying your system for eating between 70 to 80 percent raw foods, and ideally most of those will be vegetables. Vegetables provide fiber, protein, complex carbohydrates, phytonutrients, antioxidants, vitamins, and minerals that you cannot get from any other food source. There are thousands of vegetables available to us, yet we still sometimes get stuck eating the same ones, like carrots, until our palms turn orange. Out of habit or laziness, we fail to recognize there is an abundance of magnificently beautiful, flavorful, and vibrant veggies available to us, and so there should never be a cause for boredom.

Take kohlrabi, for example, also known as German turnip and a relative of brussels sprouts and broccoli. Beneath the thick and waxy skin of this knobby stem, a sweet and slightly juicy flesh is revealed that has a texture similar to that of potatoes. It is crisp and refreshing in the spring and summer months, when it is most abundant, and though it can be braised, steamed, pickled, or puréed, many find it is most enjoyable when eaten raw.

Another incredibly delicious veggie, whose gnarled appearance can be rather intimidating, is celery root. When you peel off the imperfect skin and cut away the fibrous stalk, you discover a tender and zesty center. Its versatile flesh can be enjoyed blended into soups, eaten raw, tossed with a green salad, or steamed and served with a bit of apple, which complements its flavor beautifully.

LOOK TO THE SEA FOR YOUR VEGGIES

Sea vegetables are often regarded as unpalatable, unapproachable, or too pungent in flavor, yet they are some of the most nutrient-dense foods on the planet and when prepared properly and blended with complementary ingredients, they are a savory and rich enhancement to home-cooked meals. Kombu, a type of kelp, is rich in fucoidan, a carbohydrate with anti-inflammatory properties that has been shown to aid in the prevention and reversal of some cancers.

The people documented to be among the healthiest in the world, with the longest active life spans, are the Okinawans. In addition to having a diet rich in fresh fruit, grains, and vegetables, the natives of this Japanese culture eat an abundance of kombu as well as wakame and arame seaweeds. Researchers attribute Okinawans' 80 percent lower risk of prostate and breast cancers and 50 percent lower risk of colon cancers to their overall healthy diet, consumption of fucoidan-rich foods, active lifestyle, and positive outlook.

Other sea vegetables with anti-inflammatory, anticancer, and free radical–banishing properties are spirulina and chlorella. As you learned in chapter 2, chlorella is single-celled green algae available in both convenient tablets and powdered form. It is high in protein, trace minerals, vitamins, and omega-3 fatty acids. Chlorella supports the immune system and is known for its ability to bind to pesticides, carcinogens, heavy metals, radiation, and toxins, which allows these barriers to good health to be safely and efficiently eliminated from the body.

Spirulina is versatile blue-green algae that provides more than one hundred minerals and vitamins and has a high concentration of iron, vitamin B, beta-carotene, sulfur, chlorophyll, and antioxidants. It even contains nearly 55 to 70 percent protein by weight and all essential amino acids.

Both of these nutrient-rich sea organisms can be enjoyed by blending them into smoothies, soups, dressings, and sauces, and incorporating them into main dishes, chips, snacks, anddesserts. In the recipes that follow, you will be introduced to the sometimes intimidating vegetables mentioned, will savor their tastiness, and will learn how to enjoy them consistently in your Balanced Raw diet.

ENJOY FRUIT IN MODERATION DURING THIS PHASE

Sweet fruits such as kiwi, pineapple, apples, melons, cherries, and berries are all incredibly nutritious. They provide energy, fiber, antioxidants, and phenols and are a significantly healthy contribution to a Balanced Raw lifestyle. In some cases, however, when your body's health is compromised by a weak immune system, low stomach acid, allergies, or inflammation, it is a good idea to reduce the quantity of these fruits for a short period of time because unhealthy yeast and bacteria, which feast on sugars of any kind, including the sugar in fruit, can complicate existing conditions.

During this phase, I suggest you enjoy only two servings of sweet fruits per day at most. One serving is considered ½ cup (75 g) of berries, one small apple or pear, two (3 x 1-inch, or 7.6 x 2.5-cm) pineapple spears, one medium kiwi, or one small banana. Fatty, acidic, or tart fruits such as avocado, tomatoes, lemons, and limes do not apply.

PREPARE YOUR DIGESTIVE SYSTEM FOR CLEANSING

As you learned in chapter 2, alkalizing grains such as buckwheat, millet, quinoa, and amaranth, starchy veggies such as winter squash and sweet potatoes, and legumes including beans and lentils are nutrition powerhouses and welcome in the Balanced Raw diet.

During the elimination phase, however, you will be preparing your system for accepting the light meals of the next phase, which includes only fresh pressed juices, blended smoothies, puréed soups, and salads. To properly prepare your system for acceptance of an almost entirely liquid diet, you will be eliminating all grains and legumes, and nearly all starchy vegetables during this first week. These carbohydrates all take more digestive energy to break down and when you undergo cleansing, you want digestion to be a breeze. Grains to temporarily avoid are rice, oats, quinoa, buckwheat, amaranth, millet, couscous, barley, triticale, rye, corn, and teff. In week 3, the restore phase, you will reintroduce alkalizing grains, sweet potatoes, winter squash, beans, and lentils.

ALKALIZE YOUR BODY'S PH AND WARD OFF INFECTIONS AND DISEASE

Body alkalinity is a popular topic because it has been noted that if the pH levels in your body are aptly alkaline, bacteria and infections cannot thrive and you are more resistant to major and minor diseases. This concept is not new and was first brought to light in the late 1920s by William Howard Hay, M.D.. He suggested that all disease is caused by auto-toxication, or "self-poisoning," which is developed by an accumulation of acid in the body.

Your body strives for pH balance, or the balance between acid-forming and alkaline-forming ions. This delicate balance is disrupted by overconsumption of acid-forming foods such as meat, dairy, soda, sugar, oils, and refined flours, by taking prescription drugs, and by not eating enough alkalizing foods such as fresh vegetables and fruit. The acidity causes your body to steal minerals from your organs and your bones to neutralize acidity. And as you saw earlier in this chapter, if your organs are overburdened, your body is ripe for disease and illness. Foods that promote alkalinity are:

- bok choy
- brussels sprouts
- watercress
- kohlrabi
- mustard greens
- cucumber
- squash
- lettuces
- carrots
- celery
- parsley
- spinach
- cauliflower
- celery root
- napa cabbage
- arugula
- broccoli
- zucchini
- artichokes
- romaine
- fennel
- parsnip
- beets
- chard

Alliums, which include leeks, onions, shallots, and garlic, also have alkalizing properties as do the citrus fruits grapefruit, lemons, and limes. That may sound unusual, but the citric and lactic acids in these low-sugar fruits metabolize to sodium bicarbonate when absorbed, creating an alkalizing effect. Sea vegetables such as those mentioned above also promote a more alkaline pH. During this phase you will enjoy plenty of alkaline-enhancing dishes and may find pleasure in enjoying them on a regular basis, which will stimulate good health long term.

ELIMINATION-FRIENDLY MEALS AND SEVEN-DAY DIET SUGGESTIONS

You have been shown what to eliminate from your diet; now is the time to tune in to the abundance of foods you can enjoy during the next seven days and a few extra diet tips to support you during the week.

• Consume as many of the vegetables listed above as you like and enjoy them lightly steamed, raw, or puréed.

• Every morning, within 20 minutes of rising, drink 8 ounces (235 ml) of warm water with the juice of ¹/₂ lemon. This will promote detoxification and elimination.

• In addition to the 8 ounces of warm water in the morning, try to consume an additional 20 ounces (285 to 570 ml) of fresh water to further cleanse your digestive system.

• Get at least 7 hours of sleep per night, take deep breaths throughout the day, and ensure you get a minimum of 20 minutes of exercise, even if it's light yoga, stretching, or simply going for a walk.

The following recipes have been developed to support your elimination phase and ensure you are receiving balanced nutrition from alkaline vegetables, high-fiber foods, and those with a low sugar content. They all take less than thirty minutes to prepare and are free of corn, soy, gluten, nuts, dairy products, legumes, and grains.

WEEK 1 MEAL PLAN

For optimum results, try your best to adhere to the week's meal suggestions without deviation. You may enjoy the recommended meals on different days than those outlined below. For example, if needed, the Hidden Greens Chocolate Shake for Tuesday could be swapped with Friday's Veggie Blast.

WEEKDAY	BREAKFAST	LUNCH	DINNER	SNACK
Monday	Pumpkin Spice Morning Chia Porridge	Red Cabbage, Asparagus, and Radish Slaw	Big Herb Salad with Creamy Garlic and Spirulina Dressing	Spirulina Coconut Truffles
Tuesday	Hidden Greens Chocolate Shake	Tamarind Tossed Squash Noodles	Shaved Roots and Herbed Parsnip Stack	Chili-Lime Veggie Crudité
Wednesday	Blue Greens Smoothie	Cauliflower Rice Collard Wrap with Crunchy Vegetables and Lemon-Tahini Sauce	Carrot Noodles with Bean Sprouts, Cabbage, and Miso-Ginger Sauce	Spirulina Coconut Truffles
Thursday	Pumpkin Spice Morning Chia Porridge	Celery Root and Leek Soup with Green Apple	Raw Zucchini Noodles with Fresh Tomatoes, Sun-Dried Olives, and Kale Pesto	Chili-Lime Veggie Crudité
Friday	Veggie Blast Fresh Pressed Juice	Glowing Greens and Hemp Soup	Big Herb Salad with Creamy Garlic and Spirulina Dressing	Spirulina Coconut Truffles
Saturday	Hidden Greens Chocolate Shake	Shaved Roots and Herbed Parsnip Stack	Carrot Noodles with Bean Sprouts, Cabbage, and Miso-Ginger Sauce	Chili-Lime Veggie Crudité
Sunday	Blue Greens Smoothie	Raw Zucchini Noodles with Fresh Tomatoes, Sun-Dried Olives, and Kale Pesto	Celery Root and Leek Soup with Green Apple	Spirulina Coconut Truffles

WEEK 1

RED CABBAGE, ASPARAGUS, AND RADISH SLAW WITH MUSTARD VINAIGRETTE

Crunchy and refreshing, this twist to traditional cabbage slaw is full of antioxidants and cleansing vegetables, and the Dijon vinaigrette provides a savory and pungent kick.

YIELD: 3 SERVINGS | **TIME:** 20 MINUTES (INCLUDES PREP TIME) | **EQUIPMENT:** MORTAR AND PESTLE OR SMALL FOOD PROCESSOR, SMALL MIXING BOWL, LARGE BOWL, PEELER, MANDOLINE (OPTIONAL)

INGREDIENTS:

FOR THE VINAIGRETTE:

1 large clove garlic

½ teaspoon sea salt

2 tablespoons (28 ml) red wine vinegar

1 tablespoon (15 g) organic Dijon mustard

1 tablespoon (15 ml) cold-pressed and unfiltered olive oil

3 tablespoons (45 ml) water

FOR THE SALAD:

12 medium asparagus stalks, peeled into very thin strips from end to end, then cut into 2-inch (5.1-cm) strips

8 medium red radishes, thinly sliced

1 small head red cabbage, very thinly sliced or shaved with a mandoline

½ cup (30 g) fresh parsley, chopped

¼ cup (56 g) hemp or pumpkin seeds

PREPARATION:

① To make the vinaigrette, mash the garlic and sea salt together using a mortar and pestle until you achieve a paste. Transfer to a small bowl. Mix in red wine vinegar and Dijon mustard and stir to combine. Whisk in olive oil and water until thoroughly emulsified; set aside. Alternatively, if you do not have a mortar and pestle, blend all dressing ingredients in a small food processor.

② To make the salad, in a large bowl, combine dressing, asparagus, radish, cabbage, parsley, and seeds, and toss to coat evenly. Enjoy immediately.

NOTE: This batch of slaw will stay fresh when refrigerated in an airtight, glass container for up to 3 days. Dressing will stay fresh for up to 5 days. If enjoying on multiple days, refrain from adding seeds until right before serving, as this will ensure they maintain crunch.

CAULIFLOWER RICE COLLARD WRAP WITH CRUNCHY VEGETABLES AND LEMON-TAHINI SAUCE

Enjoy the texture, flavor, and added nutrition of rice made from cauliflower. When wrapped in collard leaves with cooling vegetables and a citrusy tahini sauce, the result is a light yet filling salad roll.

YIELD: 3 ONE-WRAP SERVINGS | **TIME:** 25 MINUTES (INCLUDES PREP TIME) | **EQUIPMENT:** FOOD PROCESSOR, FINE MESH STRAINER, MEDIUM MIXING BOWL, BLENDER

INGREDIENTS:

FOR THE RICE:

1½ cups (150 g) raw cauliflower (florets only)

2 tablespoons (28 ml) brown rice vinegar

1 tablespoon (15 ml) maple syrup or agave nectar

½ teaspoon fine sea salt

FOR THE LEMON-TAHINI SAUCE:

3 medium cloves garlic

3 tablespoons (45 ml) fresh lemon juice

3 tablespoons (45 g) raw tahini

½ cup (120 ml) water

¼ teaspoon sea salt

FOR THE WRAP:

3 large collard leaves, tough ends trimmed and discarded

1 large carrot, peeled and julienned

½ medium seedless cucumber, peeled and julienned

¼ red bell pepper, stem trimmed, cored, and julienned

¼ cup (4 g) fresh cilantro leaves, roughly chopped

PREPARATION:

① To make the rice, in a food processor fitted with an S blade, pulse cauliflower until super fine and paste-like. Transfer to a fine mesh strainer and press out excess liquid.

② Transfer cauliflower to a medium mixing bowl and add brown rice vinegar, maple syrup or agave, and sea salt. Stir to combine and set aside.

③ To make the sauce, in a Vitamix or other high-speed blender, combine garlic, lemon juice, tahini, water, and sea salt. Blend until smooth and divide among ramekins for serving.

④ To assemble wraps, lay collard leaves out on a large, flat surface and fill each with one-third of the cauliflower rice. Top with a few slices each of carrots, cucumber, red bell pepper, and finish with cilantro, allowing each vegetable to peek out the ends a bit for presentation.

⑤ Holding one side (lengthwise) of the collard, wrap it over the filling and tuck under filling to secure, then finish rolling up. Using a sharp knife, cut through the middle (short ways), transfer to a serving plate, and serve with Lemon-Tahini Sauce.

NOTE: Refrigerate extra Lemon-Tahini Sauce for up to 4 days in an airtight, glass container. Rolls will stay fresh for 1 day.

RAW ZUCCHINI NOODLES WITH FRESH TOMATOES, SUN-DRIED OLIVES, AND KALE PESTO

Noodles made from raw zucchini are a welcome alternative to traditional pastas, and in this recipe, their subtle flavor is enhanced with salty olives, succulent fresh tomato, and a rich and peppery pesto.

YIELD: APPROXIMATELY 2 TO 3 SERVINGS | **TIME:** 20 MINUTES (INCLUDES PREP TIME) | **EQUIPMENT:** SPIRAL SLICER (OR A PEELER FOR PEELING THIN NOODLE RIBBONS), SMALL FOOD PROCESSOR, SMALL BOWL, LARGE MIXING BOWL

INGREDIENTS:

FOR THE PASTA:

3 medium zucchini or golden rod yellow squash, ends cut off, and each cut in half, depth-wise

FOR THE PESTO:

2 large cloves garlic

3 tablespoons (36 g) nutritional yeast

3 tablespoons (45 ml) lemon juice

3 tablespoons (45 ml) water

2 cups (110 g) kale leaves, roughly chopped

¼ teaspoon black pepper

2 tablespoons (28 g) hemp or pumpkin seeds, plus 1 tablespoon (14 g) for garnish

2 medium plum tomatoes, diced

2 tablespoons (13 g) sun-dried olives, chopped

PREPARATION:

① To create noodles, use a spiral slicer with zucchini or squash halves and transfer to a large bowl. Alternatively, if you do not have a spiral slicer you may use a peeler to achieve thin ribbons.

② To make the pesto, in a small food processor, combine garlic, nutritional yeast, lemon juice, water, kale, and black pepper, and pulse until you achieve a blended yet still textured mix. Add seeds and pulse until thoroughly blended. Transfer to a small bowl and set aside.

③ In a large mixing bowl, combine zucchini or squash noodles, pesto, tomatoes, and olives, and toss until thoroughly coated. Turn out onto plates, sprinkle with hemp or pumpkin seeds, and serve immediately.

NOTE: Zucchini noodles can be refrigerated in an airtight, glass container for up to 3 days for use in other dishes. Excess pesto will stay fresh in the refrigerator for up to 5 days.

WEEK 1

BIG HERB SALAD WITH CREAMY GARLIC AND SPIRULINA DRESSING

A large salad of fresh herbs and baby lettuces is a great way to get your daily intake of healthful greens. Tossed with a creamy and decadent garlic dressing and cool and crunchy garden vegetables, this is a complete meal in a single bowl.

YIELD: 2 SERVINGS | **TIME:** 25 MINUTES (INCLUDES PREP TIME) | **EQUIPMENT:** BLENDER, SMALL BOWL, LARGE MIXING BOWL

INGREDIENTS:

FOR THE DRESSING:

3 small cloves garlic

1 small shallot, chopped

½ teaspoon sea salt

2 teaspoons (8 g) nutritional yeast

1 teaspoon apple cider vinegar

3 tablespoons (45 ml) water

1 tablespoon (14 g) sunflower seeds

½ teaspoon spirulina powder

FOR THE SALAD:

4 cups (220 g) baby lettuces

1 large handful cilantro leaves, roughly chopped

1 large handful parsley leaves, roughly chopped

2 tablespoons (8 g) fresh dill, chopped

¼ cup (40 g) thinly sliced red onion

1 small bulb kohlrabi, peeled and thinly sliced

½ small bulb fennel, thinly shaved

Pinch of cracked black pepper

PREPARATION:

① To prepare the dressing, combine garlic, shallot, sea salt, nutritional yeast, cider vinegar, water, sunflower seeds, and spirulina powder in a Vitamix or other high-speed blender and blend until thoroughly combined. Transfer to a small bowl and set aside.

② To make the salad, in a large bowl, toss baby lettuces, cilantro, parsley, dill, red onion, kohlrabi, and fennel with dressing. Divide between plates and finish with black pepper.

NOTE: Any remaining dressing can be refrigerated in an airtight, glass jar for up to 3 days.

PUMPKIN SPICE MORNING CHIA PORRIDGE

A base of chia seeds provides volume and texture, and pumpkin pie spice brings the essence of the holidays to your bowl. Now you can have Thanksgiving any time and get a healthy dose of fiber, too!

YIELD: APPROXIMATELY THREE 1-CUP (157-G) SERVINGS | **TIME:** 30 MINUTES (INCLUDES CHILL TIME) | **EQUIPMENT:** BLENDER

INGREDIENTS:

⅔ cup (109 g) chia seeds

2 large soft-pitted deglet noor dates

1 cup (235 ml) coconut water

1 cup (235 ml) coconut milk

1 tablespoon (6.6 g) pumpkin pie spice

1 teaspoon alcohol-free vanilla extract

¼ teaspoon cinnamon

⅛ teaspoon ground ginger

2 tablespoons (28 ml) maple syrup or agave nectar

Shredded coconut or diced apple, for serving

PREPARATION:

① In a Vitamix or other high-speed blender, combine all the ingredients and blend until thoroughly smooth.

② Transfer to a glass container, and chill for at least 20 minutes before enjoying. Top with shredded coconut or diced apple before serving.

NOTE: Chia porridge will maintain its freshness when refrigerated in an airtight, glass container for up to 5 days. It can also be frozen for a cool and creamy treat.

BLUE GREENS SMOOTHIE

Sweet and tangy, this anytime smoothie is loaded with antioxidants, fiber, phenols, and omega-3 fatty acids. And it is the perfect smoothie for introducing greens into a child's diet because the tropical fruit and sweet berry flavors mask the grassiness of kale and spinach.

YIELD: APPROXIMATELY TWO 16-OUNCE (475-ML) SERVINGS | **TIME:** 5 MINUTES (INCLUDES PREP TIME) |
EQUIPMENT: BLENDER

INGREDIENTS:

1 cup (150 g) frozen mixed berries

2 cups (60 g) spinach leaves

2 cups (110 g) chopped kale leaves

2 cups (475 ml) coconut water

¼ cup (42 g) frozen pineapple bits

2 tablespoons (20.4 g) chia seeds

PREPARATION:

In a Vitamix or other high-speed blender, combine berries, spinach, kale, coconut water, pineapple, and chia seeds. Blend on high for 1 minute until thoroughly combined and serve immediately.

NOTE: Smoothie may be blended, refrigerated in glass, and enjoyed within 24 hours, but for maximum nutrient potency, sip immediately.

VEGGIE BLAST FRESH PRESSED JUICE

Move over, V8. This blend of fresh garden vegetables is unexpectedly tangy and has an extra-special boost of flavor from the addition of fresh garlic, cilantro, and sea salt.

YIELD: APPROXIMATELY TWO 16-OUNCE (475-ML) SERVINGS | **TIME:** 10 MINUTES (INCLUDES PREP TIME) | **EQUIPMENT:** JUICER

INGREDIENTS:

2 large handfuls cilantro

½ pound (225 g) spinach leaves

4 green onions

1 small clove garlic

1 medium lemon, skin cut away, pith kept intact

2 small celery stalks

4 medium plum tomatoes

2 medium carrots

¼ teaspoon sea salt

PREPARATION:

Pass all ingredients except salt through a juicer. Sprinkle in salt and serve.

NOTE: Juice may be pressed, refrigerated in glass, and enjoyed within 24 hours, but for maximum nutrient potency, sip immediately. For a refreshing and nutrient-rich virgin Bloody Mary, salt the rim of your glass and add a garnish of one celery stalk, a wedge of lemon, and two green olives. You can spice the cocktail by passing a jalapeño or red chile pepper through the juicer and then stirring in fresh grated horseradish and black pepper.

DID YOU KNOW?

The reason this veggie juice is not opaque red and does not have the same thick texture of V8 is because the store-bought variation is made from a concentrate of tomato paste and water. The Veggie Blast Fresh Pressed Juice may not look as appetizing as V8, but it's fresh and superior in taste.

CELERY ROOT AND LEEK SOUP WITH GREEN APPLE

You will not believe this soup is free of dairy because it is so creamy and rich. Green apple adds a touch of tang to the woody flavor of celery root and the sweetness of the leeks.

YIELD: APPROXIMATELY THREE 1½-CUP (355-ML) SERVINGS | **TIME:** 30 MINUTES (INCLUDES PREP TIME) | **EQUIPMENT:** SOUP POT, BLENDER

INGREDIENTS:

2 teaspoons (10 ml) coconut oil

1 large leek, washed thoroughly, tough greens discarded, and chopped

1 large clove garlic, chopped

1 medium celery root, skin peeled away and flesh cut into cubes

1 medium celery stalk, chopped

4 cups (950 ml) vegetable stock

½ teaspoon sea salt, plus a pinch, divided

¼ teaspoon ground white pepper

1 small bay leaf

1 cup (235 ml) unsweetened coconut milk

½ small green apple, diced small and placed in a bowl with water and a bit of lemon juice to keep from browning

PREPARATION:

① In a soup pot over medium-high heat, warm the coconut oil. Add the leek and garlic and heat for 2 minutes. Add the celery root and celery, and sauté until the vegetables are soft, about 6 minutes.

② Add vegetable stock, ½ teaspoon sea salt, white pepper, and bay leaf. Reduce to low, cover, and simmer for 15 minutes.

③ Uncover soup, remove bay leaf, and in batches, transfer to a Vitamix, or other high-speed blender, and purée soup. Be sure to vent blender lid and cover with a kitchen towel to avoid splatter. Return puréed soup to the cleaned soup pot over low heat.

④ Add the coconut milk to the soup and simmer for 10 minutes. Season to taste with salt and white pepper.

⑤ Divide among soup bowls and top with a small spoonful of diced green apple and a pinch of sea salt.

NOTE: This soup is also delicious served cold and can be refrigerated for up to 5 days in an airtight, glass container. Diced apples should remain in lemon water, but will still turn brown within 2 days.

GLOWING GREENS AND HEMP SOUP

Hearty Swiss chard is puréed with nutty hemp seeds, salty miso, spicy red pepper flakes, and savory aromatics to provide a nourishing soup that is rich in flavor and can be enjoyed bowl after bowl without guilt.

YIELD: APPROXIMATELY FOUR 1½-CUP (355-ML) SERVINGS | **TIME:** 30 MINUTES (INCLUDES PREP TIME) |
EQUIPMENT: SOUP POT, BLENDER

INGREDIENTS:

1 teaspoon coconut oil

1 cup (160 g) sliced sweet onion

1 medium clove garlic, minced

4 cups (950 ml) vegetable stock

4 cups (220 g) chopped green Swiss chard, ribs discarded

3 tablespoons (48 g) garbanzo (chickpea) miso

2 tablespoons (28 g) hemp seeds

¼ cup (60 ml) coconut milk

⅛ teaspoon red pepper flakes

2 teaspoons (10 ml) coconut aminos

PREPARATION:

① In a soup pot over medium-high heat, warm the coconut oil. Add the onions and garlic and heat for 2 minutes. Add the vegetable stock and bring to a low boil. Add the chard and let cook for 2 minutes.

② Turn off the heat and add the miso, hemp seeds, coconut milk, red pepper flakes, and coconut aminos. Stir to combine.

③ Transfer to a Vitamix, or other high-speed blender, tilt lid slightly, cover with a kitchen towel to avoid splattering, and blend until smooth, about 1 minute. Serve immediately.

SPIRULINA COCONUT TRUFFLES

Who says truffles can't be healthy? These morsels are smooth, buttery, and rich in flavor, and still give you a healthy dose of protein, essential fatty acids, and loads of antioxidants.

YIELD: APPROXIMATELY EIGHT 2-TRUFFLE SERVINGS | **TIME:** 20 MINUTES (INCLUDES CHILL TIME) |
EQUIPMENT: MEDIUM MIXING BOWL, CHILLED PLATE

INGREDIENTS:

½ cup (112 g) coconut butter, at room temperature (not melted and not hard)

1 cup (80 g) unsweetened shredded coconut

3 tablespoons (45 ml) maple syrup or agave nectar

2 tablespoons (16 g) raw cacao powder

1 tablespoon (8 g) spirulina powder

½ teaspoon alcohol-free vanilla extract

PREPARATION:

① In a medium mixing bowl, combine the coconut butter, shredded coconut, maple syrup or agave, cacao powder, spirulina, and vanilla extract. Mix with your hands until thoroughly combined.

② Scoop 2 teaspoons at a time into your hands and roll into a tight ball. Place on a chilled plate. Repeat until you have about 16 truffles. Transfer to the refrigerator and let chill for 10 minutes before enjoying.

NOTE: Store truffles in the refrigerator in an airtight container for up to 2 weeks. Let rest at room temperature for 5 to 10 minutes before serving.

CHILI-LIME VEGGIE CRUDITÈ

A simple snack of refreshing vegetables comes alive with spice and tang from chili powder, salt, and lime. Enjoy on-the-go or as a starter for a meal.

YIELD: 4 SERVINGS | **TIME:** 15 MINUTES | **EQUIPMENT:** SMALL BOWL

INGREDIENTS:

½ teaspoon sea salt

⅛ teaspoon cayenne pepper

¼ teaspoon chili powder

¼ teaspoon ground cumin

½ small seedless cucumber, peeled

¼ red bell pepper, stem and seeds removed

¼ medium jicama, peeled

½ small zucchini

1 large lime, halved

PREPARATION:

① In a small bowl, combine salt, cayenne, chili powder, and cumin. Stir to combine and set aside.

② Cut the cucumber, bell pepper, jicama, and zucchini into 3 x ½-inch (7.6 x 1.3-cm) sticks and place in a shallow dish. Squeeze juice of lime over all the sticks and sprinkle with the chili-salt mixture.

NOTE: Do not feel limited to just cucumber, bell pepper, jicama, and zucchini, lightly steamed sweet potato, yellow squash, asparagus, and green beans are also tasty, as is fresh kohlrabi.

SHAVED ROOTS AND HERBED PARSNIP STACK

This savory entrée is exquisite in appearance and full of fiber, antioxidants, and protein. You will love the robust herbed parsnip purée, which is layered between thin slices of lightly steamed squash and fresh tomato.

YIELD: 4 SERVINGS | **TIME:** 30 MINUTES (INCLUDES PREP TIME) | **EQUIPMENT:** VEGETABLE STEAMER, FOOD PROCESSOR, MANDOLINE

INGREDIENTS:

2 cups (220 g) peeled and cubed parsnips

1 large zucchini, peeled and shaved into disks with a mandoline

1 large yellow summer squash, peeled and shaved into disks with a mandoline

1 large celery root, peeled and shaved into disks with a mandoline

3 cloves garlic, mashed

½ teaspoon ground sage

½ teaspoon dried thyme

4 tablespoons (16 g) fresh parsley, chopped, divided

1 small shallot, minced

½ teaspoon sea salt

¼ teaspoon ground black pepper, plus a pinch for garnish

2 tablespoons (28 ml) fresh lemon juice

½ cup (120 ml) water

2 red tomatoes, thinly sliced

2 teaspoons cold-pressed and unfiltered olive oil

2 tablespoons (7.5 g) fresh parsley, chopped

PREPARATION:

① Fill the bottom of a vegetable steamer with water and bring to a boil. Steam parsnips for 12 minutes. Remove and set aside.

② Repeat with zucchini until just soft, about 30 seconds. Remove with tongs and set aside. Repeat with yellow squash, and then celery root, each about 30 seconds.

③ To make the parsnip purée, add the parsnips, garlic, sage, thyme, parsley, shallot, sea salt, and black pepper to a food processor. Pulse until combined. Add lemon juice and water, and purée until smooth.

④ To prepare layered stacks, place a slice of tomato on the center of a plate and top with a thin layer of the parsnip purée. Top the purée with a disk of celery root. Then spread another layer of purée and top with zucchini, spread another layer of parsnip purée on zucchini, and finish with a disk of squash.

⑤ Repeat one time more until you have two slices of each vegetable. Finish each stack with a few drops of olive oil, a sprinkle of sea salt, ground black pepper, and chopped parsley.

NOTE: If you do not have a mandoline, use a very sharp knife to achieve thin slices of the vegetables. To increase your daily dose of greens, steam a bit of kale, spinach, or chard for 30 seconds and add as a layer.

CARROT NOODLES WITH BEAN SPROUTS, CABBAGE, AND MISO-GINGER SAUCE

This Asian-inspired carrot noodle dish is vibrant and full of antioxidant-rich vegetables, with a sauce perfectly balanced by salt, sweet, spice, and tang.

YIELD: 4 SERVINGS | **TIME:** 25 MINUTES (INCLUDES PREP TIME) | **EQUIPMENT:** BLENDER, LARGE BOWL

INGREDIENTS:

FOR THE SAUCE:

1 clove garlic, smashed

1½-inch (3.8-cm) piece fresh ginger, chopped

1 tablespoon (15 ml) agave nectar

1 tablespoon (16 g) plus 1 teaspoon garbanzo (chickpea) miso

1 tablespoon (15 ml) plus 1 teaspoon ume plum vinegar

1 tablespoon (15 ml) plus 1 teaspoon coconut aminos

1 tablespoon (15 ml) lemon juice

2 tablespoons (30 g) tahini

¼ cup (60 ml) water

FOR THE NOODLES:

10 medium carrots, peeled, and then peeled into long ribbons from end to end

1 cup (50 g) bean sprouts

1 cup (70 g) shredded purple cabbage

¼ cup (25 g) chopped green onions, white and light green parts only

2 teaspoons (5.4 g) black sesame seeds

2 tablespoons (2 g) cilantro, chopped

PREPARATION:

① To make the sauce, in a Vitamix or other high-speed blender, combine the garlic, ginger, agave, miso, vinegar, coconut aminos, lemon juice, tahini, and water. Blend on high for 30 seconds. Set aside.

② The prepare the noodles, in a large bowl, toss the carrots, bean sprouts, cabbage, and green onions with the dressing and serve garnished with black sesame seeds and chopped cilantro.

NOTE: You can substitute zucchini or yellow squash noodles for the carrots, or make a colorful dish by combining all three. Also feel free to experiment with adding other vegetables such as baby bok choy, daikon radish, and thinly sliced red bell pepper.

TAMARIND TOSSED SQUASH NOODLES

If you have never had tamarind, you are in for a real treat. This sweet and sour condiment brightens the flavor of mellow spaghetti squash and pairs magnificently with green vegetables, subtle daikon radish, and savory cilantro.

YIELD: 4 SERVINGS | **TIME:** 30 MINUTES (INCLUDES PREP TIME) | **EQUIPMENT:** BLENDER, VEGETABLE STEAMER, LARGE BOWL

INGREDIENTS:

FOR THE DRESSING:

1 tablespoon (16 g) tamarind concentrate or paste, soaked in 2 tablespoons (28 ml) warm water

2 tablespoons (28 ml) coconut aminos

2 tablespoons (28 ml) fresh lime juice

1 small clove garlic

1 small red or green Thai chile, minced and seeds removed

2 teaspoons (28 ml) maple syrup or agave

2 tablespoons (28 ml) water

1 teaspoon sesame oil

FOR THE NOODLES:

1 medium spaghetti squash, cut through the middle lengthwise, seeds removed, and then each half cut in half widthwise

2 bunches baby bok choy

6 asparagus stalks, chopped

½ cup (58 g) peeled and julienned daikon radish

2 tablespoons (2 g) cilantro, chopped

PREPARATION:

① To make the dressing, in a Vitamix or other high-speed blender, combine the tamarind and soaking water, coconut aminos, lime juice, garlic, Thai chile, maple syrup or agave, water, and sesame oil. Blend on high for 30 seconds and set aside.

② To make the noodles, fill the bottom of a vegetable steamer with water and bring to a boil. Place the 4 quarters of the squash in a basket over the water, cover, and steam for 25 minutes.

③ Remove the squash from the basket and leave the water boiling. Let the squash cool until you are able to touch it, and then using a fork, scrape the flesh away from the skin in long shreds. Transfer to a large bowl.

④ Add the bok choy to the basket and steam for 1 minute. Remove, roughly chop, and add to the squash noodles. Add asparagus pieces to the pan and steam for 3 minutes. Remove and add to the squash noodles.

⑤ Add daikon radish and dressing to the bowl, and toss to coat. Divide among plates and garnish with chopped cilantro.

NOTE: If you cannot find tamarind concentrate or paste, blend 7 pitted prunes or dried apricots with 3 dried dates and 4 tablespoons (60 ml) lime juice in a food processor. Use in place of the 1 tablespoon (16 g) tamarind concentrate and 2 tablespoons (28 ml) soaking water.

HIDDEN GREENS CHOCOLATE SHAKE

There is no better way to get your greens than in a rich and velvety chocolate shake. You will think you are enjoying dessert for breakfast while getting a mega-dose of fiber, chlorophyll, omega-3s, and phytonutrients.

YIELD: APPROXIMATELY TWO 16-OUNCE (475-ML) SERVINGS | **TIME:** 5 MINUTES (INCLUDES PREP TIME) | **EQUIPMENT:** BLENDER

INGREDIENTS:

2 cups (60 g) spinach leaves

4 large kale leaves, ribs removed

2 tablespoons (16 g) raw cacao powder

5 drops liquid stevia (vanilla crème or chocolate flavors are extra yummy)

2 cups (475 ml) coconut water

1 tablespoon (10.2 g) chia seeds

2 large soft-pitted deglet noor dates

1 teaspoon spirulina or chlorella powder

5 or 6 ice cubes

PREPARATION:

In a high-speed blender, combine spinach, kale, cacao powder, stevia, coconut water, chia seeds, dates, spirulina, and ice, and blend for 1 minute until thoroughly combined. Serve immediately.

NOTE: This smoothie may be blended, refrigerated in glass, and enjoyed within 24 hours, but for maximum nutrient potency, sip immediately. Omit stevia and instead sweeten with half a banana for a chocolate-covered banana smoothie.

CHAPTER 5

WEEK 2 CLEANSE

RID YOUR BODY OF WASTE AND TOXINS

CLEANSE-SUPPORTING RECIPES

- Cooling Sweet Pea and Mint Soup
- Cleansing Coconut Carrot Soup
- Indian Spiced Cream of Cauliflower Soup
- Sweet Sulfur Beautifying Juice
- Hot Hot Pepper and Tomato Soup
- Citrus, Pomegranate, and Celeriac Salad
- Minty Piña Fresca
- Ruby Rabbit Pressed Juice
- Fennel, Avocado, and Rocket Salad with Lemon-Caper Vinaigrette

- Holiday Apple Pie Smoothie
- Raspberry Lime Chia Cooler
- Spiced Watermelon Tonic
- Detoxify Me Smoothie
- Heart Throb Juice
- Pretty in Pink Cabbage Salad
- Happy Belly Sprout Salad
- Mediterranean Herb Kale Salad
- Anti-Inflammatory Parsley Salad

YOU HAVE BEEN LIBERATED from artificial and processed foods and are now aware of the challenges you must navigate to achieve optimum health. You've overcome one of these barriers by stocking your pantry with only healthful foods to support your journey.

I would not be surprised if you are eager to dive into your cleanse and release the toxins that have nestled in your body for years—a comfortable environment they like to call home.

Before doing so, it is important to understand how to detox safely. Diving in without guidance can leave you cleansing inefficiently, causing illness and increased toxicity. This chapter provides you with ten steps to support you during this week's cleanse and sets you up for ongoing detoxification in the years to come.

THE TOXIC TOLL

With every passing year, your body is bombarded with toxins absorbed from drinking unfiltered water; ingesting hormones, additives, and preservatives from the foods you eat; and being exposed to chemicals in cosmetic products, household cleaners, prescription drugs, environmental poisons such as lead and mercury, and even from the air you breathe.

As you learned in the previous chapter, your liver is responsible for detoxification but already has many tasks on its plate and cannot always get to the thorough filtration of these harmful particles. As a result, they set up permanent residency in your adipose (fat) tissue and cells and, in most cases, must be forced to move out. It is essential you handle the eviction process gingerly, because the toxins tend to retaliate if not contained and when their negative effects are not neutralized. If not gently encouraged to leave the nest, they will make you sick and uncomfortable and in some cases your health will be compromised and you will be worse off than if you had just let the toxins remain in their habitat.

WHAT IS DETOXIFICATION?

Detoxification is the process of first neutralizing harmful substances (toxins) and then eliminating them through your kidneys, lungs, skin, liver, and bowels, with most of the cleansing processes taking place in your liver. Proper detoxification gives your body the opportunity to restore harmony to the functions of these organs, freeing you of unwanted weight and chronic disease.

When the liver is asked to serve during a cleanse, because it is likely already burdened with toxins it must be nourished and supported throughout every step of the process. Follow the provided nutrient recommendations and ten detox tips below and you will come through your cleanse feeling light and rejuvenated.

If, during your cleanse, you begin feeling jittery, faint, or dizzy; experience excessive diarrhea or vomiting; or have an excruciating headache, you are releasing, but not eliminating, compromising toxins, and this is a serious condition you will want to avoid. Only those effects mentioned in chapter 3, such as mild fatigue, a dull headache, mild body aches, sadness, unusual dreams, congestion, or a mild change in bowel movements, are considered normal effects of a safe cleanse.

The Two Phases to Your Detox

Two essential phases are necessary to purge, neutralize, and eliminate harmful substances from your body. During the first phase, your liver converts fat-soluble toxins into water-soluble substances so that in phase 2, these substances can easily be eliminated through your skin in the form of perspiration, your mouth and nose via breath, and through bowel excretion.

During phase 1, when your liver converts fat-soluble toxins, the process produces metabolites (small molecule by-products that result from the breakdown of toxins), and many of these metabolites are free radicals, which increase the toxic load on your body. This is why it is prudent to adhere to the provided tips so you can help these unhealthy molecules make their way out of your body efficiently, shielding you from unnecessary discomfort and further disease.

HOW TO SUPPORT YOUR LIVER DURING THE DETOX JOURNEY

You now know your liver is responsible for hundreds of bodily functions, such as processing poisons and regulating and balancing sugar, hormone, and cholesterol levels. Throw the effects of a focused detox into the mix, and now it has an even greater responsibility to neutralize, filter, and eliminate toxins before they re-enter your bloodstream and result in greater illness. Because of this, your liver needs additional support during your cleanse, and the following nutrients help to stimulate healthy liver function and encourage the flushing of toxins released into your bloodstream during cleansing. The supportive vitamins, minerals, and plant extracts described below are commonly found in supplement form while others, such as sulfur, can be obtained from food sources, some of which are included in the recipes that follow.

Milk thistle: The compound silymarin that is present in the seeds of milk thistle promotes the synthesis of glutathione, a powerful antioxidant paramount to enhancing detoxification by reducing the toxic load of free radicals in your liver during cleansing. Milk thistle also increases protein synthesis, which is an important process during detoxification. Protein combining revs chemical reactions and moves toxins through your system with greater speed and efficiency (for more information, see the sidebar "What Does Protein Have to Do with Detoxing?" on page 94). Look for milk thistle at your natural foods store, in particular one with 70 to 80 percent standardized silymarin. You will want to aim for about 300 mg each day during this week as well as during weeks 3 and 4, and you can take the capsules with food or on an empty stomach.

Dandelion root: This wondrous herb commonly found in capsule and tea form has incredible cleansing power. When used for liver health, it increases bile production, which assists in transporting toxins out of the body. It also contains many of the micronutrients required for cleansing such as magnesium, calcium, and vitamin C. During this cleansing week, sip 1 cup (235 ml) of organic dandelion root tea one to two times daily. Because dandelion root is also a diuretic, drink 1 cup (235 ml) of water for each cup of tea in addition to your regular water intake.

Vitamins B_6 and B_3 (niacin): These essential B vitamins must be present in the liver to convert carbohydrates into energy, and during your detox, efficient carbohydrate synthesis is vital. In addition to consuming B vitamin–rich foods such as cauliflower, berries, stone fruits, root vegetables, nutritional yeast, spirulina, cabbage, and spinach, which are included in the provided recipes, take a B complex sublingual tablet. Sublingual vitamins are dissolved under the tongue, making them superior to capsules. As they dissolve, their nutrient power is absorbed through the many exposed blood vessels and delivered directly to the bloodstream, bypassing the stomach, where potency would be weakened. The recommended daily minimums are 1.2 mg of B_6 and 15 mg of B_3, with four times that amount being safe to ingest without adverse reactions, according to the National Institutes of Health. During this cleansing period and the two weeks that follow, take at least 3 mg of B_6 and 30 mg of B_3. Most B complex supplements will contain B_{12}, also an essential vitamin for optimum health and one described further in chapter 7. Dissolve one tablet at a time twenty minutes before or two hours after a meal. Avoid the consumption of any liquids for twenty to thirty minutes after taking the tablet. After you have completed these remaining three weeks, reduce your intake to only the minimum recommended dose for maintenance unless suggested otherwise by your health care practitioner.

Glutathione: As mentioned in the section on milk thistle, glutathione is essential for liver detoxification. Foods rich in glutathione include watermelon, asparagus, garlic, onions, grapefruit, and avocados, all of which are included in the following recipes.

Amino acids of glutamine and lysine: These amino acids support phase 2 of your cleanse by binding to heavy metals that are released from your fat cells during phase 1. Once bound to amino acid molecules, the liver views these metals as nonthreatening and will eliminate them from your body rather than attacking them. Some very good sources of glutamine and lysine are spinach, kale, parsley, chlorella, spirulina, and hemp seeds.

Probiotics: Probiotics are microbial substances that promote the growth of healthy gut bacteria and strengthen the intestinal wall. This is important because if your intestines are plagued with weak barriers, toxins can easily enter the bloodstream. Once they do, the liver is again forced to engage them, which you want to avoid. One probiotic taken twice daily as part of your cleanse will encourage the growth of healthy bacteria, which will destroy toxins and build strong barriers. Take an enteric-coated probiotic that allows the capsule to be delivered to the small intestine safely without getting destroyed by stomach acid, and look for brands containing at least six probiotic strains, especially *Bacillus coagulans* and *Lactobacillus*. Andrew Weil, M.D., an expert in holistic healing, suggests selecting probiotics that require refrigeration because they have living bacteria cultures that help healthy gut flora grow and flourish; choosing probiotics with colony-forming units (CFUs); and taking one capsule with a meal up to three times daily during a time of cleansing or if you are ill. Following this program, take one or two probiotic capsules daily with a light meal for maintenance.

Sulfur: Another nutrient that is absolutely necessary during cleansing is sulfur. The compounds in sulfur bind to metallic toxins and other free-radical molecules and aid in their elimination. Many of the supporting recipes in this chapter and those found in chapter 4 contain sulfur-rich foods such as organic spinach, broccoli, kale, garlic, onions, radishes, cabbage, and shallots. Sulfur is also essential because you need it to produce amino acids and proteins, both of which are necessary for detoxification.

WHAT DOES PROTEIN HAVE TO DO WITH DETOXING?

Keeping with the 80:10:10 ratio, a 10 percent presence of protein in your diet during detoxing is sufficient. Plant-based proteins, rich in bioavailable, short-chain amino acids, are best for supporting the detoxification efforts of your liver. Amino acids help liver cells recognize free-roaming toxins as nonthreatening, which allows these toxins to be neutralized and converted into water-soluble molecules and safely released from the body.

This is one of the reasons why an all-juice fast or the Master Cleanse is not ideal for cleansing—both lack amino acids and protein. You will want to consume the highly absorbable amino acids found in chia and hemp seeds, raw cacao, and sea vegetables, all of which are included in the recipes you will be enjoying during your detox.

DETOX LIKE A PRO IN TEN SIMPLE STEPS

In chapter 3 you were introduced to some possible side effects of detoxing and informed of those symptoms that are nonthreatening. To help reduce the amount of discomfort you may experience during your cleanse and to ensure you not only release but also expel the toxins, follow the ten steps below.

DETOX STEP 1: ELIMINATE ALL COOKED FOODS TO ENHANCE CLEANSING

During the next week, you will avoid cooked foods. At the same time you will want to flood your body with as many minerals, enzymes, vitamins, and antioxidants as possible to support cleansing actions, and you will get an abundance of these micronutrients from uncooked food. Second, hearty foods, including those enhanced by cooking such as grains, beans, and starchy vegetables, though very healthful, require more digestive energy to break down. During cleansing, you want your energy freed up to support your liver and be less tasked by digestive activities.

DETOX STEP 2: PRACTICE INTERMITTENT FASTING FOR DEEPER DETOXIFICATION

The fast I am referring to occurs through the night between your last bite of food and your morning meal. This window of time will ideally be twelve hours.

So if you enjoy your last meal at 8:00 p.m., you should refrain from eating anything until 8:00 a.m. This is a habit you will want to adopt for life and not just during this cleansing period. This fast helps your body detoxify regularly because about eight hours after your last bite, your body completes digestive processes and enters detox mode. During the night, your digestive system works at full capacity while other systems slow down or lie dormant. Your body then requires four to five hours for detoxing, and according to cleansing experts Alejandro Junger, M.D., and John Douillard, M.D., this is done most efficiently at night.

DETOX STEP 3: BLEND YOUR MEALS TO PREDIGEST YOUR FOOD AND ENHANCE DIGESTIVE ACTIVITY

The action of blending fruits, vegetables, and seeds helps break down their fibrous cell walls, making them more absorbable and their delivery into your bloodstream quicker and more efficient. It also reduces the time and energy needed for digestion. Again, the less energy commissioned by your digestive system, the more your liver has for the purging of toxic waste.

During your cleansing week, I encourage you to enjoy only blended and puréed foods such as fresh-pressed juices, soups, and smoothies for breakfast and dinner, and for lunch a solid yet raw meal.

DETOX STEP 4: FILL UP ON FIBER TO MOVE TOXINS THROUGH YOUR BOWELS

I do not encourage an entirely juice cleanse or one where you fast for long periods of time because doing so can result in constipation from lack of fiber, and any delay in regular bowel movements creates more toxic buildup. In the cleansing phase, and for the rest of your Balanced Raw life, you will consume plenty of fiber for regularity. A sufficient intake of fiber is at least 35 grams per day. While cleansing, I encourage at least 40 grams, and the recipes provided ensure you receive this amount. For example, the **Hidden Greens Chocolate Shake** (page 89) has 23 grams of fiber in a single serving! The sources of fiber acceptable during the cleansing phase are dark leafy greens, berries, seeds, apples, sea greens, and other vegetables.

DETOX STEP 5: HYDRATE TO FLUSH YOUR ORGANS AND CELLS OF BUILT-UP TOXINS

At a minimum, drink 70 ounces (2 L) of filtered water every day. This amount should be in addition to any other liquids, including coconut water, vegetable juices, and almond milk, which are all included in the recipes.

Because your body does much of its detoxing duties at night, flush your system first thing in the morning to wash away decay. Aim to consume a minimum of 20 to 30 ounces (591 to 887 ml) of water before your first meal. To enhance the cleansing action, add fresh lemon juice to your water because lemon is an effective liver detoxifier. Also, ensure the water you consume in the morning is at room temperature to avoid shocking your system upon rising.

DETOX STEP 6: EXFOLIATE TO DEEPEN CLEANSING

Your skin loves stimulation. It is your largest organ and a powerful instrument in releasing toxins from your body. Using a dry, natural bristle brush to scrub your skin stimulates your blood vessels, increasing the flushing of waste. To effectively stimulate your skin, prior to getting in the shower, brush upward starting at the soles of your feet, then work your way up your shins and calves, behind your knees, over your thighs and buttocks, lower back and abdomen, chest, underarms, and then neck. Immediately after, shower in warm water and use an all-natural cleanser to wash away the dead skin cells and toxins.

DETOX STEP 7: ENJOY A MASSAGE FOR A MEGA TOXIN RELEASE

Sure, massage is relaxing and takes you on a temporary mind vacation, but it also stimulates your lymphatic system, which gets the poisons moving through your body rather than living stagnant in your cells. During this cleansing week, book a deep tissue or lymphatic massage (or employ a loved one to do it for you) and then try to include regular massages as part of your lifestyle following the program.

DETOX STEP 8: SHOWER TO INCREASE CIRCULATION AND STIMULATE CLEANSING

Showers are magnificent—they wake you up while relaxing your muscles and clearing your mind, and prepare you for the coming day. What you might not know is they eliminate toxins through the open pores of your skin. One way to increase this toxic elimination is to alternate between hot and cold water because this increases blood circulation and gets toxins moving. For one minute each, turn the water to as hot as you can stand and then to as cold as you can bear. Do this near the end of your shower for a few cycles and end with cold water to tighten and close your pores.

DETOX STEP 9: BE AN EFFICIENT SWEATING MACHINE AND PURGE TOXINS THROUGH YOUR PORES

One of the most effective ways your body eliminates toxins is through perspiration. I encourage you to engage in any activity that will welcome your pores to purge every single day. If you are drawn to less-intensive exercise such as yoga, try going to a hot yoga class or hot Pilates. Running is a great way to sweat and does not require a gym membership or travel time. Just tie on a good pair of running shoes and bounce out the toxins. You can also hike, walk, or even swim. Achieve balance between exerting enough to perspire while avoiding too high an intensity level, because for the next two weeks you are detoxing and restoring health and need energy reserves to support you through the process.

DETOX STEP 10: MASTER YOUR INHALES AND EXHALES FOR INCREASED DETOXIFICATION

Sounds simple, right? Although you may be taking enough shallow breaths to keep you alive, the deep inhales and exhales necessary to release toxins are likely an afterthought if you even think to breathe deeply at all. Breathing removes built-up carbon dioxide from your lungs and purifies your body by expelling toxins. Deep breathing also brings peace and tranquility to your day by calming the mind and focusing your attention on the present moment. This, too, is detoxifying because you are releasing stressful thoughts and expelling negative mind energy.

Deep breaths are those that raise and lower your stomach and lungs. Deep inhales and exhales, each lasting three seconds or more, increase circulation, calm the mind, and release stale air and toxins through the nose and mouth. During your program and beyond, make deep breathing a daily habit. A few times each day, close your eyes and breathe in slowly through your nose and then exhale out your mouth while visualizing all stress, toxins, and negative thoughts being washed away with each breath.

READY, SET, CLEANSE

One of the greatest joys of a food-assisted cleanse is that you still get to eat! And you do not eat just to survive. While you are nourishing and detoxifying your body, you will be noshing to satisfy your taste buds, too! In no way do the following cleansing dishes lack flavor, density, aroma, or stunning presentation. They have all been developed with the intent to provide vital and cleanse-enhancing nutrients, enough fiber to keep you feeling sated and your bowel movements regular, and variety and flavor to satisfy your desire to eat yummy food that keeps you from getting bored or feeling discouraged.

As mentioned before, enjoy a puréed, juiced, or blended meal for breakfast and again for dinner, and a solid yet raw meal midday. For the next seven days, select uncooked recipes from chapters 4 and 5, and try to include as much variety as possible. There are plenty of delectable soups, juices, salads, and smoothies to choose from, so you should not need to eat or drink the same dishes over and over again.

THE SKINNY ON SNACKING

Do your best to avoid between-meals snacking, as doing so creates a barrier to deep detoxification. The longer periods of fasting between each meal allow the liver, kidneys, and digestive system to direct energy to cleansing and not spend it all on digestive function.

Snacking often occurs as a result of boredom, or is a signal you are not getting enough macro- and micronutrients in your three square meals. Depending on your lifestyle and activity level, you may require a larger meal to last you through to the next one, and that is okay. Just do your best to fight the snacking urge. Sometimes going for a walk, writing, or engaging in another activity will take your mind off the need for a snack and you will realize you are not craving it anymore. However, if you find you simply cannot ignore a true hunger pain, then enjoy a single serving of a sensible snack such as the **Chili-Lime Veggie Crudité** (page 82).

WEEK 2 MEAL PLAN

For optimum results, try to adhere to the week's meal suggestions without deviation. Because of the availability of products and the demands of your schedule, you may enjoy the recommended meals on different days than those outlined below. For example, if needed, the Heart Throb Juice for Monday could be swapped with Thursday's Sweet Sulfur Beautifying Juice.

WEEKDAY	BREAKFAST	LUNCH	DINNER
Monday	Heart Throb Juice	Fennel, Avocado, and Rocket Salad with Lemon-Caper Vinaigrette and ½ cup Pretty in Pink Cabbage Salad	Cooling Sweet Pea and Mint Soup
Tuesday	Holiday Apple Pie Smoothie	Happy Belly Sprout Salad and ½ cup Pretty in Pink Cabbage Salad	Hot Hot Pepper and Tomato Soup
Wednesday	Ruby Rabbit Pressed Juice	Mediterranean Herb Kale Salad and ½ cup Pretty in Pink Cabbage Salad	Indian Spiced Cream of Cauliflower Soup
Thursday	Sweet Sulfur Beautifying Juice	Citrus, Pomegranate, and Celeriac Salad and ½ cup Pretty in Pink Cabbage Salad	Cleansing Coconut Carrot Soup
Friday	Detoxify Me Smoothie	Anti-Inflammatory Parsley Salad and ½ cup Pretty in Pink Cabbage Salad	Raspberry Lime Chia Cooler
Saturday	Minty Piña Fresca	Fennel, Avocado, and Rocket Salad with Lemon-Caper Vinaigrette and ½ cup Pretty in Pink Cabbage Salad	Indian Spiced Cream of Cauliflower Soup
Sunday	Spiced Watermelon Tonic	Happy Belly Sprout Salad and ½ cup Pretty in Pink Cabbage Salad	Hot Hot Pepper and Tomato Soup

COOLING SWEET PEA AND MINT SOUP

The delicate flavors of sweet peas and fresh mint are enhanced with nutty tahini and subtle shallots. This soup is exquisite served chilled or at room temperature.

YIELD: APPROXIMATELY THREE 1½-CUP (355-ML) SERVINGS | **TIME:** 40 MINUTES (INCLUDES PREP, THAWING, AND CHILL TIME) | **EQUIPMENT:** BLENDER

INGREDIENTS:

1 tablespoon (10 g) chopped shallots

2 cups (475 ml) vegetable stock

1 (10-ounce, 280-g) bag frozen peas, brought to room temperature

1 teaspoon sea salt

¼ teaspoon ground black pepper

2 tablespoons (30 g) raw tahini paste

¼ cup (60 ml) unsweetened almond or hemp milk

⅓ cup (32 g) fresh mint leaves, loosely packed

PREPARATION:

① In a Vitamix or other high-speed blender, combine the shallots, vegetable stock, peas, sea salt, black pepper, tahini, and almond or hemp milk.

② Blend until smooth, about 30 seconds. Add mint to blender and blend 30 seconds more. If desired, thin the soup by adding 1 tablespoon (15 ml) of vegetable stock at a time.

③ Refrigerate for 30 minutes to 1 hour before serving or enjoy at room temperature.

NOTE: For a more woodsy-flavored soup, try making this recipe with asparagus instead of peas. Use frozen asparagus tips if you can find them or substitute the same amount of fresh asparagus (bright green parts only) for the 10 ounces (280 g) of frozen peas.

WEEK 2

CLEANSING COCONUT CARROT SOUP

This soup can be enjoyed any time of the day and will leave you feeling nourished and sated. Hints of ginger and turmeric add warmth and dimension to the unexpected combination of sweet carrots and coconut.

YIELD: APPROXIMATELY FOUR 2-CUP (475-ML) SERVINGS | **TIME:** 15 MINUTES (INCLUDES PREP TIME) | **EQUIPMENT:** BLENDER

INGREDIENTS:

4 medium carrots, peeled and cubed

1½-inch (3.8-cm) piece fresh ginger

1½ cups (355 ml) coconut water

1¼ cups (295 ml) coconut milk

½ teaspoon ground turmeric

½ teaspoon fine sea salt

2 tablespoons (10 g) shredded coconut, for serving

PREPARATION:

① In a Vitamix or other high-speed blender, combine carrots, ginger, coconut water, coconut milk, turmeric, and sea salt, and blend on high until smooth, about 1 minute.

② Garnish with shredded coconut, and serve at room temperature.

NOTE: If you prefer a little heat, add 1 teaspoon hot curry powder, ½ teaspoon ground cumin, and ¼ teaspoon cayenne pepper with all other spices.

INDIAN SPICED CREAM OF CAULIFLOWER SOUP

Enjoy an ethnic twist to traditional cream of cauliflower soup. Spices of cumin, curry, cinnamon, and nutmeg warm you from the inside, building digestive fire that enhances detoxification.

YIELD: APPROXIMATELY THREE 2-CUP (475-ML) SERVINGS | **TIME:** 15 MINUTES, PLUS 4 HOURS (INCLUDES SOAKING TIME) | **EQUIPMENT:** BLENDER

INGREDIENTS:

3 cups (300 g) cauliflower florets

½ cup (112.5 g) pumpkin seeds, soaked for 4 hours and drained

1 tablespoon (15 ml) cold-pressed and unfiltered olive oil

4 large soft-pitted deglet noor dates, soaked for 20 minutes in warm water and drained

1 tablespoon (15 ml) lemon juice

2 cups (475 ml) vegetable stock

½ teaspoon ground cumin

½ teaspoon curry powder

¼ teaspoon ground coriander

⅛ teaspoon ground cinnamon

⅛ teaspoon ground nutmeg

½ teaspoon sea salt

¼ teaspoon ground white pepper

⅛ teaspoon ground cloves

2 tablespoons (2 g) cilantro, chopped, for serving

PREPARATION:

In a Vitamix or other high-speed blender, combine all the ingredients except the cilantro. Blend on high until smooth, about 2 minutes. Garnish with chopped cilantro and serve at room temperature.

NOTE: Another delightful way to enjoy this creamy soup is to omit the cumin, curry, coriander, cinnamon, nutmeg, cloves, and cilantro. Instead, add one small garlic clove, 1 teaspoon fresh thyme, 1 small shallot, and 1 tablespoon (2.6 g) fresh chopped basil leaves to the blender. Garnish with chopped fresh parsley, toasted pumpkin seeds, and fresh cracked pepper.

SWEET SULFUR BEAUTIFYING JUICE

No need to worry; it doesn't taste or smell like sulfur, despite the abundance of this amazing mineral being poured into your glass. Sulfur is a superior skin saver, aids in liver health, and supports fat digestion and assimilation. The flavors of sulfur-rich watercress and radish are mellowed by sweet grapes, peppery ginger, cool cucumber, and fresh mint.

YIELD: APPROXIMATELY ONE 16-OUNCE (475-ML) SERVING | **TIME:** 5 MINUTES (INCLUDES PREP TIME) |
EQUIPMENT: JUICER

INGREDIENTS:

½ **bunch watercress**

1½-**inch (3.8-cm) piece fresh ginger**

1 **large handful mint leaves**

3 **romaine leaves**

1 **medium lemon, peeled, pith kept intact**

4 **medium red radishes, scrubbed**

1 **cup (150 g) red grapes**

½ **cucumber**

PREPARATION:

Pass all the ingredients through a juicer and enjoy.

NOTE: If you do not have grapes, substitute other sweet fruits such as pear, red apple, cantaloupe, or pineapple. Freeze the juice to enjoy later if you are not going to drink it immediately.

DID YOU KNOW?

This is a powerful detox tonic because of the use of two mega sulfur-containing ingredients—watercress and radishes. Sulfur supports protein synthesis and the compounds in this cleanse-supporting nutrient bind to heavy metals and free radicals, aiding in their elimination.

HOT HOT PEPPER AND TOMATO SOUP

This raw tomato soup has some serious kick from dried chile flakes and cayenne pepper. The properties of these hot additions speed metabolism and promote healthy detoxification.

YIELD: APPROXIMATELY FOUR 2-CUP (475-ML) SERVINGS | **TIME:** 20 MINUTES (INCLUDES SOAKING TIME) |
EQUIPMENT: BLENDER

INGREDIENTS:

4 medium plum tomatoes, chopped

¾ medium red bell pepper, cored and chopped

2 small shallots, chopped

2 medium celery stalks with greens, chopped

½ cup (80 g) chopped sweet onion

2 medium cloves garlic

½ teaspoon dried chile flakes

¼ teaspoon cayenne pepper

1 teaspoon sea salt

1 teaspoon ground cumin

1 teaspoon curry powder

½ teaspoon ground coriander

1 tablespoon (15 ml) lemon juice

2 cups (475 ml) coconut milk

1 cup (235 ml) water

6 sun-dried tomatoes, soaked for 20 minutes in hot water and drained

2 tablespoons (2 g) cilantro, chopped, for serving

PREPARATION:

In a Vitamix or other high-speed blender, combine all the ingredients except the cilantro and blend on high until smooth, about 2 minutes. If desired, thin with coconut milk or water, a little bit at a time, until desired consistency is achieved. Serve at room temperature with a sprinkle of chopped cilantro.

NOTE: For a smoky tomato soup, omit curry powder and ground coriander, increase cumin to 2 teaspoons (5 g), and add 2 dried chipotle peppers that have been reconstituted in ¼ cup (60 ml) warm water for 20 minutes. Add the soaking water as well as the peppers, and blend and serve as instructed above.

CITRUS, POMEGRANATE, AND CELERIAC SALAD

Get ready for a mouthwatering and crunchy salad packed with antioxidants and alkalizing goodness. Celeriac is often underappreciated or overlooked because of its gnarly facade, but its insides reveal a cool, crisp, and grassy flesh that plays nice with juicy pomegranate and tangy citrus.

YIELD: APPROXIMATELY FOUR 1-CUP (55-G) SERVINGS | **TIME:** 20 MINUTES (INCLUDES PREP TIME) | **EQUIPMENT:** MEDIUM BOWL, MANDOLINE OR SHARP KNIFE, PEELER, SMALL BOWL, LARGE MIXING BOWL

INGREDIENTS:

2 tablespoons (28 ml) fresh lemon juice, divided

2 medium celeriac (celery roots), ends trimmed, peeled

2 tablespoons (28 ml) fresh orange juice

2 teaspoons (10 ml) maple syrup or agave nectar

2 tablespoons (28 ml) cold-pressed and unfiltered olive oil

2 teaspoons (10 ml) white wine vinegar (such as champagne)

½ teaspoon sea salt

¼ teaspoon black pepper

1 large celery stalk with greens, stalk julienned and greens minced

2 medium navel oranges, peeled and broken into segments

¼ cup (56 g) pomegranate seeds

PREPARATION:

① Prepare a medium bowl of water with 1 tablespoon (14 ml) of the lemon juice. Cut the celery root into matchsticks using a knife or mandoline, and submerge in lemon water.

② In a small mixing bowl, combine orange juice, remaining 1 tablespoon (14 ml) lemon juice, maple syrup or agave, olive oil, vinegar, sea salt, and pepper. Stir to combine.

③ Drain celery root, and transfer to a large mixing bowl. Toss with celery, celery greens, orange segments, pomegranate seeds, and dressing. Serve immediately.

NOTE: This salad can also be made using fresh grapefruit segments, which add a tangier dimension to the dish than the sweet orange. Green apple and green grapes are also delightful substitutions.

WEEK 2

MINTY PIÑA FRESCA

Sip on this island-inspired mocktail and let digestive enzymes do their cleansing work. Calming mint, sweet coconut water, and tangy lime juice pair beautifully with enzyme-rich and succulent pineapple.

YIELD: APPROXIMATELY ONE 16-OUNCE (475-ML) SERVING | **TIME:** 5 MINUTES (INCLUDES PREP TIME) |
EQUIPMENT: BLENDER

INGREDIENTS:

1 cup (235 ml) coconut water

1 cup (165 g) fresh or frozen pineapple chunks

¼ cup (24 g) mint leaves, packed

Juice of 1 lime, about 2 tablespoons (28 ml)

4 or 5 ice cubes

PREPARATION:

In a Vitamix or other high-speed blender, combine coconut water, pineapple, mint, lime, and ice. Blend for 30 seconds and enjoy.

NOTE: Fresca may be blended, refrigerated in glass, and enjoyed within 24 hours. Alternatively, pour into ice pop molds for a healthful frozen dessert.

DID YOU KNOW?

There is more to pineapple than its sweet and succulent juice and flavor. It contains bromelain, an enzyme that breaks down proteins into smaller molecules, aiding in digestion. According to the University of Maryland Medical Center, South Americans have been enjoying this tropical fruit for centuries to reduce inflammation and treat indigestion. To boost digestive activity, delight in fresh pineapple prior to a meal or immediately after for dessert.

WEEK 2

RUBY RABBIT PRESSED JUICE

Aptly named, this succulent carrot juice gets it ruby hue from fresh beets and has a tangy flavor profile from the addition of red grapefruit. This juicy delight contains peppery ginger, which reduces inflammation, and beets, which detoxify and oxygenate the blood.

YIELD: APPROXIMATELY ONE 16-OUNCE (475-ML) SERVING | **TIME:** 10 MINUTES (INCLUDES PREP TIME) |
EQUIPMENT: JUICER

INGREDIENTS:

½-inch (1.3-cm) piece fresh ginger, unpeeled

2 celery stalks

1 medium red beet, scrubbed and trimmed

1 medium ruby red grapefruit, peeled, pith kept intact

5 medium carrots, scrubbed and trimmed

PREPARATION:

Pass the ginger, celery, beet, grapefruit, and carrots through a juicer. Enjoy immediately.

NOTE: Pressed juices may be frozen and enjoyed at a later time. You can also pour the juice into ice cube trays and enjoy sucking on the cool cubes throughout the day.

DID YOU KNOW?

Beet juice is a powerful blood purifier and aids in the development of red blood cells. According to scientist Mikhail Tombak, Ph.D., this ruby juice improves the structure of blood and has been shown to reduce and prevent diseases of the circulatory and digestive systems.

You can have too much of a good thing, however. Beets are incredibly efficient at purifying your system, and the toxins released by their cleansing action must filter through your liver. But as you have learned, your liver is burdened with many activities and may not be able to process heavy metals fast enough, which can result in toxic buildup. To prevent such a condition, limit your beet intake to only one per day.

WEEK 2

FENNEL, AVOCADO, AND ROCKET SALAD WITH LEMON-CAPER VINAIGRETTE

This salad is light and simple, and perfect for cleansing. Rocket, also known as arugula, has antifungal, antiviral, and antibacterial properties; boosts the immune system; and is full of vitamins and minerals. The peppery leaf gets along famously with buttery avocado and licorice-like fennel.

YIELD: 2 SERVINGS | **TIME:** 5 MINUTES (INCLUDES PREP TIME) | **EQUIPMENT:** MANDOLINE OR SHARP KNIFE, BLENDER, LARGE MIXING BOWL

INGREDIENTS:

FOR THE DRESSING:

2 tablespoons (17 g) capers

2 tablespoons (28 ml) lemon juice

2 small cloves garlic

½ teaspoon sea salt

¼ teaspoon ground black pepper

1 tablespoon (4 g) fresh parsley leaves

1 tablespoon (15 g) raw tahini paste

2 tablespoons (28 ml) white wine vinegar

1 tablespoon (15 ml) water

FOR THE SALAD:

1 large fennel bulb, ends trimmed, and shaved very thin with a mandoline or sharp knife

3 cups (60 g) rocket (arugula)

1 avocado, peeled, pitted, and cut into small cubes

PREPARATION:

① To make the dressing, in a Vitamix or other high-speed blender, combine all the dressing ingredients and blend on high for 30 seconds. Set aside.

② To make the salad, in a large mixing bowl, toss fennel, rocket, avocado, and dressing. Serve immediately.

NOTE: The vinaigrette stores nicely in airtight glass for up to 5 days in the refrigerator.

WEEK 2

HOLIDAY APPLE PIE SMOOTHIE

If you have a sudden hankering for dessert but do not want the guilt, then you are in luck. This smoothie combines the essence of holiday baking with the nourishing properties of fresh fruit, stimulating spices, and omega-rich chia. I bet you can smell the aroma of fresh-baked apple pie right this minute.

YIELD: APPROXIMATELY ONE 20-OUNCE (570-ML) SERVING | **TIME:** 5 MINUTES (INCLUDES PREP TIME) | **EQUIPMENT:** BLENDER

INGREDIENTS:

1 small sweet apple, chopped

¼ banana

½ teaspoon ground cinnamon

⅛ teaspoon ground cloves

⅛ teaspoon ground nutmeg

2 soft-pitted deglet noor dates

1 tablespoon (10.2 g) chia seeds

1 teaspoon alcohol-free vanilla extract

2 cups (475 ml) unsweetened vanilla almond milk

Pinch of sea salt

PREPARATION:

Using a Vitamix or other high-speed blender, combine all the ingredients and blend for 1 minute on high. Enjoy chilled or at room temperature.

NOTE: This smoothie makes a delightful frozen dessert. Just divide between freezer-safe containers and enjoy as a frozen custard.

DID YOU KNOW?

The use of dates in this and other recipes provides more than just sweet taste. Dates are highly nutritious morsels with anti-inflammatory, antibacterial, and antioxidant activity. They are rich in calcium, zinc, potassium, and vitamin A and are an excellent source of iron. If you struggle with anemia, be sure to include dates in your diet to help bring iron levels back into a healthy range.

Look for soft fresh dates in the produce or refrigerator sections of your market and store them in a sealed container in your refrigerator for up to 3 months.

WEEK 2

RASPBERRY LIME CHIA COOLER

This creamy and refreshing beverage is bursting with sweetness, tang, and texture. What's more, the addition of fresh raspberries promotes fat loss, and coconut water keeps you hydrated! Woo-hoo!

YIELD: APPROXIMATELY ONE 16-OUNCE (475-ML) SERVING | **TIME:** 10 MINUTES (INCLUDES PREP TIME) | **EQUIPMENT:** BLENDER

INGREDIENTS:

1 cup (125 g) raspberries

1 medium lime, juiced, about 2 tablespoons (28 ml)

1 tablespoon (10.2 g) chia seeds

1 cup (235 ml) coconut water

¼ cup (60 ml) coconut milk

5 ice cubes

PREPARATION:

Using a Vitamix or other high-speed blender, combine all the ingredients and blend for 1 minute on high. Enjoy immediately.

NOTE: Another excellent recipe for a frozen dessert. You can pour this blend into ice pop molds and lick your way to whole health!

DID YOU KNOW?

Chia seeds (yes, as in the Chia Pet) are a relative of the mint family and one of the most nutrient-dense foods available to us. These powerful little seeds have been enjoyed in South America for thousands of years and were revered by ancient warriors for promoting energy sustainability and hydration. Chia seeds offer a perfect 3:1 omega-3 to omega-6 ratio, 35 percent dietary fiber by weight, loads of antioxidants, and all the essential amino acids, making them a complete protein.

When combined with liquid, they expand to nine times their size, providing volume and emulsification for smoothies, dressings, puddings, and other desserts. When mixed with juice or coconut water, they create a refreshing tonic that increases and helps maintain hydration.

SPICED WATERMELON TONIC

There is more to watermelon than its sweet and refreshing flavor and summertime nostalgia. Believe it or not, this watery fruit is an excellent liver detoxifier and rich in antioxidants. When paired with cleansing lime juice and heart-healthy red chiles, the flavor is exquisite and its health benefits are superior.

YIELD: APPROXIMATELY ONE 16-OUNCE (475-ML) SERVING | **TIME:** 5 MINUTES (INCLUDES PREP TIME) |
EQUIPMENT: JUICER

INGREDIENTS:

½ **medium red chile pepper, core and seeds removed**

1 **small handful fresh cilantro**

1 **small handful fresh mint**

1 **medium lime, skin cut away, pith kept intact**

3 **cups (450 g) chopped fresh watermelon (with seeds)**

⅛ **teaspoon sea salt**

PREPARATION:

Pass chile pepper, cilantro, mint, lime, and watermelon through juicer. Transfer to a glass and stir in sea salt. Enjoy immediately.

NOTE: You can use these same ingredients to make a refreshing chilled watermelon soup. Follow the instructions as outlined, divide between two soup bowls, and garnish with a drizzle of coconut milk, a few drops of balsamic vinegar, fresh chopped cilantro, and a pinch of sea salt.

DETOXIFY ME SMOOTHIE

Alternating both pressed and blended juices is a good idea for balanced nutrition. Pressed juices deliver nutrients directly to your bloodstream, while blended smoothies are rich in fiber. This smoothie can be enjoyed daily and has just enough sweetness from the apple, coconut water, and dates that you won't cringe at the mega dose of greens.

YIELD: APPROXIMATELY ONE 20-OUNCE (570-ML) SERVING | **TIME:** 10 MINUTES (INCLUDES PREP TIME) |
EQUIPMENT: BLENDER

INGREDIENTS:

1 cup (235 ml) coconut water

2 cups (60 g) spinach

4 kale leaves

1 medium carrot, chopped

1 medium celery stalk, chopped

1 medium apple, cored and chopped

2 soft-pitted deglet noor dates

1 tablespoon (15 ml) fresh lemon juice

¼ bunch parsley

5 or 6 ice cubes

PREPARATION:

Using a Vitamix or other high-speed blender, combine all the ingredients and blend for 1 minute on high. Enjoy immediately.

NOTE: You may refrigerate this smoothie for up to 24 hours in an airtight glass bottle, but ideally, enjoy it immediately for maximum nutrient benefit. You can customize this smoothie by using ingredients you have on hand. Leafy greens such as chard, beet greens, dandelion, or mâche can be used interchangeably with kale and spinach, and beets stand in well for carrots, as does cucumber for the celery. Also feel free to swap pineapple, mango, pear, peaches, banana, or any other sweet fruit for the apple, and if you have powdered greens, throw them in to make your smoothie a one-of-a-kind.

WEEK 2

HEART THROB JUICE

Did you know jalapeño is exceptional for heart health? It increases circulation and reduces inflammation. In this unique juice, orange and apple are spiked with heart-healthy pepper and blended with fresh greens for a hefty dose of antioxidants.

YIELD: APPROXIMATELY ONE 16-OUNCE (475-ML) SERVING | **TIME:** 5 MINUTES (INCLUDES PREP TIME) |
EQUIPMENT: JUICER

INGREDIENTS:

1 large handful cilantro

3 cups (90 g) spinach leaves

½ medium jalapeño, stem and seeds removed

1 lime, peeled, pith kept intact

1 medium orange, peeled, pith kept Intact

1 small red apple, cored

PREPARATION:

Pass all the ingredients through a juicer and enjoy immediately.

NOTE: For a tangier blend, substitute ruby red grapefruit for the orange. Also, you may use any greens you have on hand, such as kale, chard, or dandelion.

WEEK 2

PRETTY IN PINK CABBAGE SALAD

Think sauerkraut deluxe! With the distinct flavors of garlic, ginger, cumin, and coriander, and a hint of red beet, this is no ordinary sauerkraut. It stands tall and proud, knowing it is scrumptious paired with a meal or all on its own. This versatile delight requires 10 days to ferment, but the flavor, texture, and health benefits are worth the wait.

YIELD: 4 SERVINGS | **TIME:** 15 MINUTES, PLUS 10 DAYS FERMENTATION TIME | **EQUIPMENT:** MANDOLINE OR FOOD PROCESSOR, BLENDER, 4 MASON JARS, PLASTIC SANDWICH BAGS, KITCHEN TOWELS, LARGE MIXING BOWL

INGREDIENTS:

FOR THE BRINE:

4 cups (950 ml) water

2-inch (5.1-cm) piece fresh ginger, grated

2 cloves garlic

4 teaspoons (24 g) sea salt

1 teaspoon cumin seeds

1 teaspoon coriander seeds

FOR THE CABBAGE SALAD:

1 head purple cabbage, shredded with a mandoline or in a food processor

1 medium red beet, peeled and cut into thin matchsticks

PREPARATION:

① To make the brine, in a blender, combine water, ginger, garlic, sea salt, cumin seeds, and coriander seeds. Blend for 1 minute and reserve.

② To make the cabbage salad, in a large mixing bowl, combine shredded cabbage, beets, and brine and, using your hands (be sure to wear gloves), thoroughly massage the liquid into the cabbage.

③ Divide the salad among 4 large mason jars and tightly pack each, leaving about 2 inches (5.1 cm) of space from the mouth of the jars. Ensure there are no air bubbles in the liquid and if you see any, use a kebab skewer or other thin device to pack the cabbage and remove the air. The liquid should cover the cabbage, so if you need more, make another half batch of the brine and divide among jars.

④ The cabbage needs to stay tightly packed for 7 days. To do so, press a sandwich bag into the mouth of each jar. Fill each bag with water until the water is just below the mouth of the jar. Seal the bag. This will serve as a weight.

⑤ Store the jars in a safe and dark place, out of your way and in an environment that will remain at a steady 65°F to 70°F (18°C to 21°C). Drape each jar with a kitchen towel (do not apply a lid) and let rest for 7 days.

⑥ Pull jars from storage and transfer to refrigerator. Keep the water weights intact and drape lightly with towels. Allow to refrigerate an additional 3 days, then remove towels and water weights, and apply a lid to each jar.

NOTE: Refrigerate in an airtight glass jar for use within 30 days.

WEEK 2

HAPPY BELLY SPROUT SALAD

Sprouts are incredibly nutritious but are often considered unappetizing. To liven them up, this recipe calls for a marinade of fresh lemon juice, tart plum vinegar, salty miso, and a hint of sesame. The sprouts are then tossed with crisp greens and buttery avocado, and topped with a scoop of Pretty in Pink Cabbage Salad.

YIELD: 2 SERVINGS | **TIME:** 15 MINUTES (INCLUDES PREP TIME) | **EQUIPMENT:** SMALL BOWL, MEDIUM BOWL, LARGE BOWL

INGREDIENTS:

FOR THE DRESSING:

1 tablespoon (15 ml) fresh lemon juice

2 teaspoons (10 ml) ume plum vinegar

½ teaspoon red wine vinegar

2 teaspoons (10 ml) coconut aminos

1 teaspoon garbanzo (chickpea) miso

1 teaspoon sesame oil

FOR THE SALAD:

1 cup (50 g) lentil sprouts

½ cup (25 g) mung bean sprouts

2 cups (110 g) shredded romaine

½ cup (70 g) peeled and diced cucumber

1 cup (55 g) mixed baby greens (e.g., bok choy, mesclun, chard)

1 avocado, seeded and cubed

¼ cup (4 g) cilantro, chopped, divided

1 teaspoon black sesame seeds, divided

1 cup (142 g) Pretty in Pink Cabbage Salad, divided (page 124)

PREPARATION:

① To make the dressing, in a small bowl, combine lemon juice, ume plum vinegar, red wine vinegar, coconut aminos, chickpea miso, and sesame oil. Whisk until smooth and set aside.

② To make the salad, in a medium bowl, toss lentil and bean sprouts with 1 tablespoon (15 ml) dressing and let rest for 5 minutes.

③ In a large bowl, toss romaine, cucumber, baby greens, and remaining dressing.

④ Divide romaine mixture between 2 plates, and top with lentil and bean sprouts, avocado, cilantro, and sesame seeds, and finish each with a ½ cup (71 g) scoop of Pretty in Pink Cabbage Salad.

NOTE: The kinds of sprouts you can use are not limited to only lentil and mung bean. There are so many varieties that are delicious in this dish, including adzuki, black-eyed pea, and even those made from chickpeas. For a super nutrient boost, toss in sunflower, radish, or broccoli sprouts, pea shoots, or micro greens.

MEDITERRANEAN HERB KALE SALAD

The essence of the Mediterranean is often characterized by brilliant blue waters, a light breeze, powdery sandy beaches, and cuisine made with fresh herbs, lemon, garlic, vegetables, and olive oil. This salad is no stranger to the isles and captures the flavors you would expect on a vacation to this romantic region.

YIELD: 2 SERVINGS | **TIME:** 15 MINUTES (INCLUDES PREP TIME) | **EQUIPMENT:** BLENDER, FOOD PROCESSOR, LARGE MIXING BOWL

INGREDIENTS:

FOR THE DRESSING:

2 cloves garlic

½ teaspoon sea salt

2 tablespoons (28 ml) fresh lemon juice

1 teaspoon ground cumin

1 teaspoon dried thyme

½ teaspoon ground black pepper

1 teaspoon maple syrup

2 tablespoons (30 g) raw tahini paste

¼ cup (60 ml) water

FOR THE SALAD:

2 cups (60 g) spinach

2 cups (110 g) chopped kale

½ cup (30 g) fresh parsley

¼ cup (24 g) fresh mint

¼ cup (4 g) fresh cilantro

½ cup (55 g) grated carrot

½ cup (70 g) diced cucumber

½ cup (90 g) diced tomato

¼ cup (25 g) pitted and chopped kalamata or sun-dried olives

PREPARATION:

① To make the dressing, in a blender, combine garlic, sea salt, lemon juice, cumin, thyme, black pepper, maple syrup, tahini, and water, and blend until smooth. Set aside.

② To make the salad, in a food processor fitted with an S blade, combine spinach, kale, parsley, mint, and cilantro, and pulse four or five times until finely chopped. Transfer to a large bowl.

③ Add carrots, cucumber, tomatoes, olives, and dressing to bowl, and toss to coat evenly. Serve immediately.

NOTE: Refrigerate any extra salad dressing in a glass jar with a tight-fitting lid for up to 4 days. This dressing is excellent tossed with beans or heirloom tomatoes, or served over lightly steamed or grilled zucchini.

ANTI-INFLAMMATORY PARSLEY SALAD

Parsley is a wondrous herb with anti-inflammatory, heart-healthy, and immune-boosting properties. Not only is it notably nutritious, but it is also "pleased as parsley" when paired with capers, garlic, sea salt, onions, and pumpkin seeds.

YIELD: 3 SERVINGS | **TIME:** 15 MINUTES (INCLUDES PREP TIME) | **EQUIPMENT:** FOOD PROCESSOR, BLENDER, LARGE MIXING BOWL

INGREDIENTS:

FOR THE DRESSING:

2 cloves garlic, minced

½ cup (120 ml) lemon juice

1 tablespoon (15 ml) cold-pressed and unfiltered olive oil

½ teaspoon sea salt

3 tablespoons (26 g) capers

3 tablespoons (42 g) pumpkin seeds

FOR THE SALAD:

2 bunches curly parsley leaves (4 to 5 cups, or 240 to 300 g)

2 medium white onions, diced

2 cups (270 g) English or Persian cucumbers, peeled and diced

Pinch of ground black pepper

PREPARATION:

① To make the dressing, in a Vitamix or other high-speed blender, combine all the dressing ingredients and blend until smooth, about 30 seconds. Set aside.

② To make the salad, in a food processor fitted with an S blade, pulse parsley until finely chopped. Transfer to a large mixing bowl. Add dressing, onions, and cucumbers and toss until coated. Season with black pepper.

NOTE: This salad gets better with time as the flavors develop, so you may freely store and enjoy within 3 days.

CHAPTER 6

WEEK 3
RESTORE

WELCOME BACK COOKED FOODS AND TEST FOR THOSE THAT MAY CAUSE DISCOMFORT

RESTORE-SUPPORTING RECIPES

- Asparagus Ribbons with Lentils and Citrus Vinaigrette

- Steamed Collard Rolls with Falafel and Mint Chutney

- Salt and Flame Kale Chips

- Moroccan Cauliflower and Sweet Potato Stew

- Thai Buckwheat Noodle Soup

- Quinoa, Carrot, and Currant Bowl

- Fiesta Millet Salad with Smoky Avocado Cream

- Cool Dill-icious Zucchini Ribbon Pasta

- Curried Cucumber and Coconut Toss

- Creamed Zucchini Soup

- The Balanced Raw Burger

- Za'atar Crusted Parsnip Chips

- Body-Loving Lemon Bars

- Van-Hemp-Nilla Bites

- Sugar Potato, Fiery Mushroom, and Chipotle Crème Tacos with Zesty Radish Slaw

- Parsnip Rice Sushi with Sweet Tamarind Dipping Sauce

HALLELUJAH! You completed your seven-day cleanse and although I'm sure it wasn't easy, my hope is that it was transformative! Now is the time to check in with yourself and see how you are feeling. Pull out your journal and write down any mood changes and physical sensations or observations you have had. Ask yourself questions such as:

- Am I experiencing more restful sleep? Do I feel more alert upon rising? Am I less irritable?

- Am I thinking more clearly?

- Has congestion, gas, or bloating subsided?

- Did I lose a few pounds?

- Am I craving whole and nourishing foods instead of the junk I may have been eating before?

- Which foods and meals made me feel my best?

Ponder and record what comes up for you and then go celebrate your accomplishment! Treat yourself to a relaxing massage, book a reflexology foot treatment, try an acupuncture session, buy a new outfit to honor your weight loss, or go out for a high-quality and celebratory meal (for dining tips, see the sidebar on page 138). Do something to pat yourself on the back and reward yourself for your commitment and hard work.

This restoration week is paramount to discovering which foods are illsuited for your body. Taking note of the positive changes from cleansing, as well as any lingering discomforts, will be helpful in evaluating your progress and give you something to compare this coming week's notes with.

INTRODUCE POTENTIAL ALLERGENS TO EVALUATE THEIR EFFECT ON YOUR BODY

This restoration phase is exciting because this is when you examine how certain foods affect your body. If you find that you react negatively, you can either completely eliminate them from your diet or reduce the frequency with which you consume them.

During the next seven days, you will reintroduce the foods best known to promote discomfort one at a time. Ingesting these foods in isolation is the only way to know whether they cause an adverse reaction. Testing these foods apart from other known allergens will help you discover:

- Which foods, if any, make you uncomfortable or cause an inflammatory body response

- Whether that food is causing a severe allergic, or mildly sensitive, reaction

- The level of discomfort caused by that food, whether mild to none, bearable, or severe

- Whether the food should be completely eliminated from your diet or enjoyed in moderation and on special occasions

- How to cope if the food must be eliminated

DISCOVER THE FOODS THAT ARE MAKING YOU UNCOMFORTABLE

In chapter 4, I discussed the five most common sensitivity-promoting foods—corn, soy, gluten, dairy, and nuts. In addition to these, you may have unknowingly experienced sensitivity to foods in the nightshade family. Studies show some people experience joint or arthritic pain and inflammation because of their inability to process alkaloids, a naturally occurring compound in nightshades, the Solanaceae plant family that includes bell peppers, tomatoes, cayenne, eggplant, gooseberries, tomatillos, chile peppers, goji berries, and potatoes. In addition, some people experience stomachaches and cramping shortly after eating these foods. This is because those same alkaloids interfere with nerve activity, causing spasms in the stomach.

Very few recipes in this book contain nightshades, as I do not see them as necessary to include during this four-week program and since consuming nightshades causes me to become congested, I use them sparingly. Even though, compared to the top five allergens, these foods are often regarded as nonthreatening, it can't hurt to test your physical response to them during this week.

I am not an advocate of dairy after Caldwell B. Esselstyn, M.D., and T. Colin Campbell, Ph.D., showed that casein, the protein in dairy, promotes heart disease, diabetes, and cancer. In addition, multiple studies suggest that dairy is responsible for bone loss, just the opposite of what we have been told for decades through advertising and marketing campaigns. A June 2000 study published in the *American Journal of Public Health* showed women who consumed dairy products on a regular basis experienced more bone fractures than women who avoided or rarely consumed such animal products. The science behind this bold claim states that the presence of dairy, or any animal protein for that matter, requires the body to extract calcium from bones to accompany the protein on its digestive journey. Unfortunately, after your body has assimilated the protein, the calcium used as an escort is expelled through urine and not reunited with your bones.

Even still, you may choose to include some dairy products in your diet. If so, during this week I advise you to introduce dairy-containing foods in isolation (not with any other known allergen) and monitor your reaction for forty-eight hours. Be keen to symptoms of bloating, gas, lower abdomen cramping, congestion, stomach gurgling, or diarrhea, which are the most common side effects of a dairy sensitivity.

Gluten is also an allergen I suggest avoiding, but again, you may wish to include some gluten-containing pastas, tortillas, breads, and cereals in your diet. As you reintroduce these foods, be aware of your body experiencing fatigue, depression, joint pain, headaches, gas, brain fog, or constipation, all of which have been linked to gluten sensitivity.

UNCOVER POTENTIAL ALLERGENS WITH A SIMPLE STEP-BY-STEP GUIDE

During the previous two weeks your body underwent a cleansing and repair period as you limited food intake, rid your diet of garbage food, and detoxified with nourishing soups, salads, juices, and smoothies. Your body is now in a refreshed and more balanced state, which makes now the optimal time for testing your response to potential allergens.

Every day this week you will enjoy both raw and cooked foods, and will be eating three solid meals per day rather than two liquid meals. You may, however, opt to continue with smoothies or juice in the morning rather than a solid breakfast. You will also be introducing one isolated allergen every other day and will monitor your body's response for a forty-eight-hour period. To track for at least twenty-four hours and ideally forty-eight is essential because some foods cause immediate discomfort whereas others may cause a delayed reaction, such as disruptions in sleep, feelings of agitation or lack of focus, or constipation the following day. The process of documenting your response to each food will extend into next week because allowing a day to pass between allergens for all those needing to be evaluated will require ten to twelve days. To proceed systematically, answer each evaluation question according to the following scale for sensitivity.

- A response of "great" means you have a mild or nonexistent sensitivity.

- A response of "okay" likely means you have a bearable to moderate sensitivity.

- A response of "awful" means you may have a strong sensitivity or full-blown allergy to the food.

With each known allergen, and for each day of testing, evaluate and track the following in your journal:

Note of caution: If you have a known severe allergy, please do not proceed with introducing that food.

Evaluation 1: How did you feel right after eating?

- **Great:** Full of energy, sated, alert, and content.

- **Okay:** Experienced mild gas, congestion, or fatigue.

- **Awful:** My skin was itchy, I was completely exhausted, had diarrhea, shortness of breath, tightness in my throat or chest, stomach cramps, headache, or a rash.

Evaluation 2: How did you sleep the night after eating the potential allergen?

- **Great:** Fell asleep with ease, had pleasant dreams, stayed sleeping until the morning.

- **Okay:** Fell asleep with ease, but tossed and turned and woke in the night.

- **Awful:** Had difficulty falling asleep, was hot and/or sweaty, had nightmares, tossed and turned frequently, and woke often.

Evaluation 3: How was your visit to the bathroom the morning following consumption?

• **Great:** Emptied my bowels and urinated without any problems.

• **Okay:** Had a bowel movement, but unlike other mornings, had difficulty going, was left feeling like I did not empty my colon completely, had smelly gas or feces.

Other considerations: Did you sense unusual body or urine odor? Did your urine smell of tin, copper, metal, or "off" in any other way? Was your body odor or breath offensive or unusual?

• **Awful:** Constipated and unable to go, passed lots of gas, had cramping, diarrhea, nausea, felt unrelieved.

Evaluation 4: How was your general mood and energy the day following consumption of the potential allergen?

• **Great:** Got out of bed with ease and felt rested, energized, and alert, and enjoyed all of my daily activities. I was focused and engaged, and my attitude was positive and relaxed.

• **Okay:** I engaged in normal activities but was easily annoyed or agitated. I was distracted, could not concentrate, and lacked patience and focus. Waking up and moving about was difficult, and I felt I needed a stimulant to get me going.

• **Awful:** I felt like I had a hangover, lacked motivation, felt depressed, tired, groggy, my brain was foggy, and I was anxious, nervous, and agitated. I did not want to do anything except sleep and/or eat.

Provided below are suggestions for adding in the specific foods during your test days:

Day 1: Add frozen, boiled, or grilled corn to any meal.

Day 3: Avoid consuming corn on this day and add cheese to any meal or eat one small yogurt.

Day 5: Avoid all dairy products and add steamed edamame, soy sauce, tamari, or tofu to any meal.

Day 7: Avoid all soy products and sprinkle any type of nut (almond, peanut, pistachio) on a dish or eat a small handful as a snack. It is possible you could be allergic to one type of nut and not another, so you may want to try testing each kind every other day, again in the absence of all other allergens to rule out any possiblity of allergic response.

Day 9: Avoid all nuts and introduce nightshades into your diet by including a hot chile, jalapeño, ground cayenne, or fresh tomato in a dish.

Day 11: Avoid all nightshades and include half a slice of bread or $1/2$ cup (70 g) of pasta (ensure the food contains gluten) with any meal.

MAKE SENSE OF YOUR REACTIONS SO YOU CAN AVOID THE FOODS THAT CAUSE DISCOMFORT

If the reaction you had to the food was immediate, such as in the case of a rash, shortness of breath, tight chest, or diarrhea, it is likely the food introduced in isolation is responsible for the reaction and is causing an allergic response. If you had a more mild response, such as fatigue or a headache, it is possible it was the food, but other factors may have contributed, such as stress in your day, eating too fast, eating while on the go, or experiencing a disturbing interaction or conversation while eating, so it is important you always test the food a second time and for another forty-eight-hour period.

Test the same food back to back without skipping a day in between. Respond to the same five questions to monitor your reactions and compare the answers to those from test day 1. This exercise for each known allergen should help you define your level of sensitivity to that particular food, if any.

If, for any one of the foods, your reaction was "great," then that food is likely not an issue, but alternatively if your response was "okay" or "awful" two days in a row, you may want to eliminate or reduce consumption.

LEARN HOW TO EAT WITH CAUTION AND AWARENESS

Once the week is completed and you have tested the top five food allergens and if you opted to include nightshade testing as well, you should now have a pretty solid idea of the foods that harm you and those that make you feel good inside. With this knowledge comes eating discipline and self-control.

Let's say you have an "okay" (bearable) reaction to gluten. Do you want to live in a state of bearable, moderate comfort every day? I didn't think so. I am guessing you want to feel good every day with bounds of energy and your systems functioning optimally. Alternatively, do you mind feeling mild discomfort once in a while when the trade-off is pleasure during a special occasion or social experience? Perhaps. So going forward, if you wish to indulge in gluten, or any of the foods that cause you discomfort, you can now go into the eating experience knowing it may cause you mild discomfort, but that if you do not make a habit of consuming the potential allergen regularly, the discomfort will be temporary and will subside. This way, you can eat with pleasure and not fear or guilt. You will know exactly what you are getting yourself into and exactly how to get yourself out.

That said, if you had a more "awful" (severe) response, you will likely want to eliminate that food from your diet. The symptoms that correlated with these criteria are detrimental to your health, increase inflammation, contribute to weight gain, and disrupt all functions of the body. In most cases, these reactions would define the food as an allergen and not just a sensitivity-promoting food. It is best to steer clear and find a desirable alternative.

LETTING GO OF POTENTIAL ALLERGENS AND HOW TO ADOPT ALTERNATIVES

Most of us have emotional attachments to foods, especially those that cause some level of physical discomfort. We often do not first recognize the discomfort until after the comfort period. After we indulge, we'll say, "Oh, why did I eat that? My stomach is killing me!" Too often we find a way to rationalize eating these foods, by subconsciously believing they will bring us pleasure, comfort, joy, or fulfillment. But in almost all cases, when they bring these sensations, they are only temporary.

Letting go of these comforting foods may be very difficult, but the long-term reward is so much more satisfying than that of the present moment. From now on, stop before you eat. Ask yourself why you are reaching for that food that will ultimately cause you discomfort. In most cases, if you listen, you will know it is to satisfy an emotional need, not a physical one, and it should be easier to avoid. In some cases, as mentioned above, you may opt to proceed with eating the food, knowing full well what you are getting yourself into.

I have one more bit of advice about eating or avoiding certain foods. Some people find that if they experience a sensitivity to a particular food, but begin a regime of probiotics and digestive enzymes, they are able to include that food after a time without discomfort. (See page 180 for specifics on probiotics usage.) Give yourself at least three months to experience life without these foods, and if you miss them so terribly and want to include them regularly in your diet, explore this supplemental protocol, and then test the foods again using the guidelines above.

Do not despair. If you have found you have one or two or multiple allergies or sensitivities, there is an abundance of alternative foods, and I have listed some favorites in the table below.

HOW TO WELCOME COOKED FOODS INTO YOUR DIET

Hooray for cooked foods! After learning in chapter 2 about their health benefits and nourishing properties, aren't you excited to bring them back into your eating plan? It would be a shame to delay the pleasure of enjoying these fiber-rich and soul-warming foods any longer! So don't. Starting today, and for the next seven days, include cooked foods in either your lunch or your dinner. This will ease you into becoming familiar with, and including, cooked fare in the Balanced Raw diet. After that, you will be prepped for bringing cooked foods into every meal, except if you opt to keep breakfast reserved for smoothies and juices, which is just fine.

GROUP	COMMON FOODS	ALTERNATIVE FOODS
Dairy	milk, cheese, yogurt, ice cream	rice, almond, hemp, and coconut milks, cheeses, yogurts, and ice creams
Gluten	breads, refined flour, pasta, pizza crust, spelt, farro, wheat berries, cereals, barley, rye, couscous, triticale, wheat, flour tortillas	millet, gluten-free oats, flax cereal, teff bread, quinoa pasta as well as the whole grain and flakes, buckwheat groats and noodles, corn tortillas, amaranth, flours ground from rice, chickpeas, or coconut, and pizza crusts and crackers made with corn or rice
Soy	tofu, tamari, nama shoyu, soy sauce, tempeh, Bragg aminos, soybeans, soy milk, soy frozen treats, edamame	chickpeas, peas, white beans, black beans, bean patties, chickpea falafel, almond, coconut, hemp, or rice milks and frozen treats, coconut aminos, coconut jerky
Corn	corn chips, corn tortillas, polenta, hominy, masa	millet, amaranth, rice, quinoa, or rice tortillas, sweet potato, parsnip, or beet chips
Nuts	trail mix, peanuts, almonds, cashews, pistachios, Brazil nuts, and walnuts, nut butters, nut pâtés, dessert crusts, crackers, cookies	seeds such as pumpkin, sesame, chia, flax, and hemp, seed dessert crusts, coconut, coconut butter, seed spreads

THE DINING OUT DILEMMA

As you work to discover foods that provoke sensitivities or an allergic reaction, you may feel inclined to isolate yourself from social interactions to avoid falling into temptation. However, there is no need to be a recluse when more restaurants are offering allergy-free dishes or at the very least, salads, soups, sides, and even entrées that do not promote sensitivity.

If you have the ability to choose where to dine out, select places that serve plant-based and allergen-free options, such as Lebanese, Persian, Greek, Indian, Peruvian, and Thai restaurants. Many Spanish and Mexican establishments also support an allergen-free diet. If you cannot choose your venue, be a gracious guest no matter where you go and just know there is always something you can enjoy even if you need to ask your server for help with creating a special meal. Waitstaff are increasingly more familiar with unique dietary needs and will usually welcome your requests and creativity.

Whether you have selected the eatery or someone else has made dining arrangements, make a habit of scanning the menu for selections that support your transition, like a Thai green papaya salad or Indian lentil soup, or a dish made from a base of beans or vegetables, such as chana masala or curry. To avoid snacking on complimentary pita, naan, or egg rolls (which all contain gluten), order a side of brown or basmati rice, quinoa, steamed vegetables, or braised greens as soon as you sit down. Having these friendly foods in front of you will keep you from reaching for those that may bring discomfort later.

During this restoration period, decide which meal is best suitable for the inclusion of cooked food. Perhaps it is lunch where you may want more sustenance or dinner when you have more time to spend preparing the dish. Whichever it is, include just a single serving of cooked grains, starchy vegetables, or legumes. A serving of cooked grain or legumes is about $1/2$ cup (83 g), and with starchy vegetables, up to 1 cup (225 g) is acceptable. If you choose to have a cooked soup or stew, enjoy $1^1/2$ to 2 full cups (355 to 475 ml), and if you opt to have steamed leafy greens or other non-starchy vegetables, you may eat to your heart's content.

Adhere to the recommended cooking methods of steaming, grilling, or simmering. Use the accompanying recipes for inspiration, and cook only produce that is in season. That means if it is spring, grill some asparagus spears, and if it is fall, select pumpkin or brussels sprouts. Doing so will not only help you learn to eat with the seasons, but it is also more cost-effective because produce in season, in addition to being more widely available, is more reasonably priced.

Browse through all the recipes in chapters 4 through 6 and note those inclusive of cooked foods. For example, in the **Fiesta Millet Salad with Smoky Avocado Cream** (page 152), the only cooked ingredient is millet, whereas all the other components and the dressing are made from raw vegetables and seeds. This is an ideal dish for this phase. Nearly all recipes in this chapter are made with some cooked ingredients and should help transition you into the healthy world of Balanced Raw.

WEEK 3 MEAL PLAN

For optimum results, try your best to adhere to the week's meal suggestions without deviation. Because of the availability of certain foods and the demands of your schedule, you may enjoy the recommended meals on different days than those outlined below. For example, if needed, the Curried Cucumber and Coconut Toss for lunch on Tuesday could be swapped with Friday's Cleansing Coconut Carrot Soup.

WEEKDAY	BREAKFAST	LUNCH	DINNER	SNACK
Monday	Heart Throb Juice (week 2)	Cool Dill-icious Zucchini Ribbon Pasta	Asparagus Ribbons with Lentils and Citrus Vinaigrette	Body-Loving Lemon Bars
Tuesday	Hidden Greens Chocolate Shake (week 1)	Curried Cucumber and Coconut Toss	Steamed Collard Rolls with Falafel and Mint Chutney	Salt and Flame Kale Chips
Wednesday	Detoxify Me Smoothie (week 2)	Parsnip Rice Sushi with Sweet Tamarind Dipping Sauce	Moroccan Cauliflower and Sweet Potato Stew or Creamed Zucchini Soup	Van-Hemp-Nilla Bites
Thursday	Veggie Blast Fresh Pressed Juice (week 1)	Citrus, Pomegranate, and Celeriac Salad and ½ cup Pretty in Pink Cabbage Salad (week 2)	Fiesta Millet Salad with Smoky Avocado Cream	Za'atar Crusted Parsnip Chips
Friday	Ruby Rabbit Pressed Juice (week 2)	Cleansing Coconut Carrot Soup (week 2)	Sugar Potato, Fiery Mushroom, and Chipotle Crème Tacos with Zesty Radish Slaw	Body-Loving Lemon Bars
Saturday	Blue Greens Smoothie (week 1)	Fennel, Avocado, and Rocket Salad with Lemon-Caper Vinaigrette (week 2)	Thai Buckwheat Noodle Soup	Salt and Flame Kale Chips
Sunday	Holiday Apple Pie Smoothie (week 2)	Raw Zucchini Noodles with Fresh Tomatoes, Sun-Dried Olives, and Kale Pesto (week 1)	The Balanced Raw Burger	Van-Hemp-Nilla Bites

ASPARAGUS RIBBONS WITH LENTILS AND CITRUS VINAIGRETTE

Peeling thin ribbons is a delicate preparation for enjoying raw asparagus, and when they are met with buttery French lentils and a bright citrus vinaigrette, the result is a vibrant and nourishing spring salad.

YIELD: 3 SERVINGS | **TIME:** 25 MINUTES (INCLUDES PREP TIME) | **EQUIPMENT:** MEDIUM SAUCEPAN, VEGETABLE PEELER, LARGE BOWL OF ICE WATER, SMALL BOWL

INGREDIENTS:

FOR THE LENTILS:

½ cup (96 g) dried French du Puy green lentils

2 cups (475 ml) water

⅛ teaspoon sea salt

1 tablespoon (2.4 g) fresh thyme, minced

1 bay leaf

1 clove garlic, minced

FOR THE DRESSING:

1 clove garlic, minced

2 tablespoons (20 g) thinly sliced shallots

2 tablespoons (28 ml) fresh orange juice

2 tablespoons (28 ml) fresh lemon juice

1 tablespoon (15 ml) champagne vinegar

¼ teaspoon sea salt

¼ teaspoon ground black pepper

FOR THE SALAD:

1 pound (455 g) (bunch) fresh asparagus, tough ends removed

2 tablespoons (28 g) raw pumpkin seeds

1 tablespoon (6 g) each fresh mint and parsley leaves, chopped

PREPARATION:

① To make the lentils, in a medium saucepan, bring lentils, water, sea salt, thyme, bay leaf, and garlic to a boil, reduce heat to low, and cook uncovered for 20 to 25 minutes, or until al dente (not mushy, with a slight "bite"). Remove from heat and let stand in cooking liquid until all other preparations have been made.

② To prepare dressing, combine garlic, shallots, orange juice, lemon juice, champagne vinegar, sea salt, and black pepper in a small bowl and whisk until thoroughly combined. Set aside.

③ To make the salad, while lentils are cooking fill a large bowl with ice water. Wash and dry the asapargus and remove the hard ends. Lay each asparagus stalk flat on a cutting board. Using a vegetable peeler, shave the asparagus into thin ribbons from end to end. As you shave, transfer the ribbons to the bowl of ice water.

④ Drain asparagus and lentils, remove bay leaf, and return both to a large bowl. Add desired amount of dressing, pumpkin seeds, mint, and parsley, and toss to coat evenly. Enjoy at room temperature.

NOTE: Any remaining dressing can be refrigerated in an airtight glass container for use within 3 to 4 days. To add another dimension of flavor, include thinly shaved fennel.

STEAMED COLLARD ROLLS WITH FALAFEL AND MINT CHUTNEY

INGREDIENTS:

FOR THE FALAFEL:

1½ cups (246 g) cooked chickpeas

¼ cup (24 g) each fresh mint and parsley leaves

½ cup (80 g) chopped red onion

2 small cloves garlic

¼ to ½ teaspoon cayenne pepper

½ teaspoon each ground cumin and coriander

1 teaspoon sea salt

¼ cup (60 ml) water

FOR THE MINT CHUTNEY:

½ cup (8 g) fresh cilantro, packed

1 cup (96 g) fresh mint, packed

1 medium jalapeño, stem and seeds removed, roughly chopped

1 teaspoon sea salt

¼ white onion, roughly chopped

2 tablespoons (28 ml) lemon juice

¼ cup (60 ml) water

FOR THE ROLLS:

3 very large collard leaves

1 plum tomato, thinly sliced

¼ cucumber, thinly sliced

1 handful mixed greens

¼ cup (60 ml) Lemon-Tahini Sauce (see page 67)

Frequently, collard wraps are served raw and, for some people, can be difficult to digest. Quickly steaming the hearty leaves increases digestibility and creates a more interesting flavor profile.

YIELD: 3 ONE-ROLL SERVINGS | **TIME:** 25 MINUTES (INCLUDES PREP TIME) | **EQUIPMENT:** FOOD PROCESSOR, BLENDER, LARGE VEGETABLE STEAMER, 4 RAMEKINS

PREPARATION:

① To make the falafel, add all the falafel ingredients to a food processor fitted with an S blade. Purée until a smooth dough consistency is achieved, about 2 minutes.

② To make the chutney, add all the chutney ingredients to a Vitamix or other high-speed blender and blend until smooth, about 30 seconds. Use a plunger if needed to get the herbs moving and add more water, 1 tablespoon (15 ml) at a time, until you achieve a silky condiment. Divide among 4 ramekins for serving.

③ To make the rolls, wash collard leaves and trim stems to an even edge. Bring water to a boil in the bottom of a large vegetable steamer. One at a time, place collard leaves in steamer basket, cover, and steam for 30 seconds. Remove carefully with tongs to avoid tearing the leaves, and let rest on a cutting board.

④ To assemble rolls, working one leaf at a time, gently spread falafel dough over the entire leaf. Top with 2 or 3 slices of tomato, 3 or 4 slices of cucumber, a few mixed greens, and a generous drizzle of Lemon-Tahini Sauce. Tuck in the bottom and top edges of the leaf and wrap like a burrito. Cut in half, and serve immediately with mint chutney for dipping.

NOTE: The chutney can be made in advance and refrigerated in an airtight glass container for use within 3 days. You can use the chutney in a variety of ways. For example, for a unique sweet and savory treat, quickly grill pineapple or watermelon and serve topped with a small dollop of the chutney.

SALT AND FLAME KALE CHIPS

The distinct woodsy flavor of kale is mellowed with salty miso, fiery Thai chiles, and tangy plum vinegar in this anytime nutritious snack.

YIELD: 10 SERVINGS | **TIME:** 15 MINUTES, PLUS 10 HOURS (INCLUDES PREP AND DEHYDRATING TIME) | **EQUIPMENT:** BLENDER, DEHYDRATOR, PARAFLEXX SHEETS, LARGE BOWL

INGREDIENTS:

¼ cup (56 g) pumpkin seeds

2 teaspoons (10 ml) ume plum vinegar

2 teaspoons (10 ml) coconut aminos

¼ cup (60 ml) warm water

¼ cup (63 g), plus 1 tablespoon (16 g) garbanzo (chickpea) miso

1¼-inch (3.2-cm) piece fresh ginger

1 red Thai chile, stem and seeds removed, and chopped

1 large bunch green curly kale, washed, de-ribbed, dried, and broken into 2-inch (5.1-cm) pieces

PREPARATION:

① In a Vitamix or other high-speed blender, combine pumpkin seeds, plum vinegar, coconut aminos, water, miso, ginger, and chile. Blend until smooth, about 30 seconds.

② In a large bowl, combine kale and dressing, and using clean hands, massage the dressing into each leaf until they are evenly coated.

③ Divide between ParaFlexx sheets and dehydrate at 105°F (40.5°C) for about 10 hours, or until sufficiently crispy. Store in an airtight glass container for up to 2 weeks, if you can make them last that long!

NOTE: If you do not have a dehydrator, you can bake the kale chips for 30 to 40 minutes in a 250°F (121°C) oven. Check them every 5 to 10 minutes, removing those that are crispy. You lose a bit of the nutrient value with baking, but they are still a better snack alternative to chips bought at the store. To make a delicious salad, omit heating, mix in some chopped celery and grated daikon radish, and top with sesame seeds and sprouts.

MOROCCAN CAULIFLOWER AND SWEET POTATO STEW

The spices of Morocco are deeply nourishing and soothing to the soul. Starchy cauliflower and sweet potatoes soak up the fragrant aromatics in this hearty stew and are enhanced by buttery garbanzo beans, sweet peas, and fresh cilantro.

YIELD: APPROXIMATELY FOUR 1½-CUP (355-ML) SERVINGS | **TIME:** 30 MINUTES (INCLUDES PREP TIME) | **EQUIPMENT:** LARGE SAUCEPAN

INGREDIENTS:

1 teaspoon coconut oil

¼ cup (40 g) diced yellow onion

2 small cloves garlic, minced

1 tablespoon (6 g) minced fresh ginger

½ medium sweet potato, peeled and cut into 1-inch (2.5-cm) cubes

1 medium carrot, peeled and roughly chopped

½ head cauliflower, broken into small florets, about 2 to 3 cups (200 to 300 g)

1 teaspoon turmeric

⅛ teaspoon ground cloves

¼ teaspoon ground ginger

1 teaspoon ground cumin

2 teaspoons (4 g) curry powder

½ teaspoon sea salt

¼ cup (60 ml) vegetable stock

1 cup (235 ml) coconut milk

2 Roma or plum tomatoes, chopped

1 cup (164 g) cooked chickpeas

½ cup (65 g) frozen peas

¼ cup (4 g) fresh cilantro, chopped

PREPARATION:

① Heat coconut oil in a large saucepan over medium heat. Add onion, garlic, and ginger, and sauté for 2 minutes. Add sweet potato and carrot, and stir to coat, about 1 minute.

② Add cauliflower, turmeric, cloves, ginger, cumin, curry, and sea salt, and heat 1 minute. Pour in vegetable stock, coconut milk, and tomatoes. Bring to a low boil, cover, and simmer for 10 minutes.

③ Stir in chickpeas, peas, and cilantro, and warm for 5 minutes more. Divide among bowls and serve immediately.

NOTE: If you make a larger batch, this recipe lasts 4 to 5 days refrigerated in an airtight glass container. I recently brought this stew to a Super Bowl party, and it was by far the most popular dish there. Make a large batch and share the love at a potluck or other group event.

THAI BUCKWHEAT NOODLE SOUP

INGREDIENTS:

2 lemongrass stalks

2 medium kaffir lime leaves

2 small cloves garlic

1-inch (2.5-cm) piece fresh galangal (or ginger), peeled and thinly sliced

3 small Thai red chiles, stem and seeds removed, and chopped

½ teaspoon sea salt

1 teaspoon coconut oil

1 large white onion, cut into 1-inch (2.5-cm) squares

7 cups (1.7 L) vegetable stock

1 (8-ounce, 225-g) package 100 percent buckwheat noodles

2 tablespoons (28 ml) coconut aminos

2 tablespoons (28 ml) agave nectar or maple syrup

2 tablespoons (28 ml) fresh lime juice

4 medium plum tomatoes, quartered

1 cup (71 g) small broccoli florets

1 cup (150 g) snow peas, ends trimmed, and cut in half

½ cup (8 g) fresh cilantro leaves, roughly chopped

Tom Yum soup is a brothy staple identified by the blend of lime leaf, lemongrass, chiles, cilantro, and galangal, which make it a well-liked hot and sour soup. To build a complete meal, I adopted the basics of this recipe but added silky buckwheat noodles and crisp Asian vegetables for heartiness.

YIELD: APPROXIMATELY SIX 2-CUP (475-ML) SERVINGS | **TIME:** 30 MINUTES (INCLUDES PREP TIME) | **EQUIPMENT:** MORTAR AND PESTLE, LARGE SAUCEPAN

PREPARATION:

① Chop the lemongrass, reserving the fleshy center. Cut lime leaves into thin ribbons. Using a mortar and pestle, bruise lemongrass, lime leaves, garlic, galangal or ginger, Thai chiles, and sea salt into a thick paste and set aside.

② Heat coconut oil in a large saucepan over medium heat. Add onion and cook for 2 minutes. Add chile paste and stir for 30 seconds.

③ Add vegetable stock and bring to a boil. Add buckwheat noodles and cook for 6 minutes. Reduce heat to medium-low, and add coconut aminos, agave nectar or maple syrup, lime juice, tomatoes, and broccoli. Cover and simmer for 2 to 3 minutes, or until broccoli is bright green. Add snow peas, cover, and simmer for 1 minute. Stir in cilantro and serve immediately.

NOTE: Another traditional Thai soup is tom kha, which is a coconut milk–based soup. To achieve this creamier delight, reduce the vegetable stock by 2 cups (475 ml) and substitute with coconut milk.

WEEK 3

QUINOA, CARROT, AND CURRANT BOWL

I do not know what it is about grains and fruit, but they sure like each other, and in the case of tart currants, they play well with grassy quinoa. The addition of carrots and a sweet and tangy dressing with a touch of heat provides balance to this unique and satisfying grain bowl.

YIELD: APPROXIMATELY THREE 1½-CUP (355-ML) SERVINGS | **TIME:** 30 MINUTES (INCLUDES PREP TIME) | **EQUIPMENT:** SMALL BOWL, MEDIUM SAUCEPAN, LARGE MIXING BOWL

INGREDIENTS:

FOR THE DRESSING:

1 red jalapeño

2 cloves garlic, minced

1 tablespoon (15 ml) apple cider vinegar

1 tablespoon (15 ml) maple syrup

2 tablespoons (28 ml) fresh lemon juice

¼ cup (60 ml) coconut water

1 teaspoon hot paprika

2 teaspoons ground cumin

½ teaspoon sea salt

FOR THE SALAD:

1 cup (196 g) dried quinoa, rinsed well

2 cups (475 ml) water

¼ teaspoon sea salt

3 medium carrots, peeled and chopped into ¼-inch (6-mm) pieces

¼ cup (38 g) dried currants

2 tablespoons (18 g) pine nuts

¼ cup (20 g) unsweetened shredded coconut

3 tablespoons (3 g) fresh cilantro, minced

PREPARATION:

① To make the dressing, remove the stem and seeds from the jalapeño and then mince. In a small bowl, combine jalapeño, garlic, apple cider vinegar, maple syrup or agave, lemon juice, coconut water, paprika, cumin, and sea salt. Stir to combine and set aside.

② To make the salad, in a medium saucepan, combine quinoa, water, and sea salt. Bring to a boil, reduce heat to low, cover, and simmer for 12 minutes. Remove from heat, keep covered, and let rest for 5 minutes. Fluff with a fork and transfer to a large mixing bowl.

③ Add carrots, currants, pine nuts, shredded coconut, dressing, and cilantro to bowl and toss all ingredients until thoroughly combined. Serve immediately.

NOTE: Experiment by making this grain salad with fresh chopped mango or grilled stone fruits such as peaches or nectarines. Fresh pitted cherries are also delicious in place of currants, as are chopped dried or fresh figs. If you don't have maple syrup, agave nectar works just as well in this recipe.

FIESTA MILLET SALAD WITH SMOKY AVOCADO CREAM

Millet has a mildly sweet and polenta-like flavor and is delightful when served with smoky chipotle peppers and sweet and tangy veggies such as jicama, red bell pepper, and chayote squash.

YIELD: APPROXIMATELY FOUR 1½-CUP (225-G) SERVINGS | **TIME:** 1 HOUR (INCLUDES PREP AND CHILL TIME) | **EQUIPMENT:** BLENDER, MEDIUM SAUCEPAN, LARGE BOWL

INGREDIENTS:

FOR THE DRESSING:

½ **large avocado, peeled and pitted**

2 **large cloves garlic**

½ **cup (120 ml) fresh lime juice**

6 **tablespoons (90 ml) water**

2 **teaspoons (5 g) ground cumin**

2 **tablespoons (28 g) hemp seeds**

1 **teaspoon sea salt**

1½ **teaspoons chipotle powder**

FOR THE SALAD:

½ **cup (50 g) dried millet**

1¼ **cups (295 ml) vegetable stock**

½ **medium red bell pepper, stem and seeds removed, and diced**

½ **large cucumber, peeled and diced**

2 **tablespoons (20 g) minced red onion**

1 **large scallion, white and light green parts only, chopped**

¼ **cup (33 g) peeled and diced jicama**

1 **chayote squash, seeds removed and diced**

¼ **cup (4 g) fresh cilantro leaves, minced**

PREPARATION:

① To prepare the dressing, combine avocado, garlic, lime, water, cumin, hemp seeds, sea salt, and chipotle powder in a Vitamix or other high-speed blender and blend until smooth, about 30 seconds. Set aside.

② To make the salad, bring millet and vegetable stock to a boil in a medium saucepan. Reduce heat to low, cover, and simmer for 25 minutes. Remove from heat, remove lid, and let the millet stand 5 minutes more. Fluff with fork and transfer to a large bowl. Refrigerate 30 minutes to 1 hour before mixing in the other ingredients.

③ Remove from refrigerator and add remaining ingredients and dressing. Toss until thoroughly mixed and serve.

NOTE: Chayote squash is a pear-shaped gourd known for its sweet and celery-like flavor and crunchy texture. Look for it in late summer and early fall. During other seasons, substitute with zucchini or yellow squash. Also, if you don't have chipotle powder, you can use 2 reconstituted dried chipotle peppers (see note on page 106 for instructions).

COOL DILL-ICIOUS ZUCCHINI RIBBON PASTA

Fresh dill is a magnificent herb for pairing with zucchini. When blended with nutty tahini and a hint of heat, the dill sauce for this raw ribbon pasta is uniquely creamy yet refreshing.

YIELD: APPROXIMATELY TWO 2-CUP (510-G) SERVINGS | **TIME:** 30 MINUTES (INCLUDES PREP TIME) |
EQUIPMENT: BLENDER, BAMBOO OR KEBAB SKEWER, PEELER, LARGE MIXING BOWL

INGREDIENTS:

2 tablespoons (30 g) tahini

¼ cup (60 ml) water

2 tablespoons (28 ml) fresh lemon juice

1 teaspoon coconut aminos

1 teaspoon sea salt

3 tablespoons (12 g) fresh dill, chopped

¼ teaspoon red chile flakes

3 medium zucchini, bottoms trimmed and dark skin peeled, stem kept intact

½ medium golden summer squash, diced

8 cherry tomatoes, halved

1 medium carrot, peeled and julienned

½ medium red bell pepper, stem and seeds removed, diced

PREPARATION:

① In a Vitamix or other high-speed blender, purée tahini, water, lemon juice, coconut aminos, salt, dill, and red chile flakes. Blend for 30 seconds until smooth, and set aside.

② One at a time, press a skewer lengthwise through the center of each zucchini leaving 1 to 2 inches (2.5 to 5.1 cm) sticking out of the stem for you to hold on to. Use the peeler to shave long thin ribbons, end to end, until the seeds begin to show. At that point, stop peeling and reserve the core of zucchini for a soup such as Creamed Zucchini Soup (see p. 159). Transfer zucchini ribbons to a large mixing bowl.

③ Add squash, tomatoes, carrot, and red bell pepper to bowl. Pour in dill dressing and toss to coat. Divide among plates and enjoy.

NOTE: This recipe has so many options for variance. You may opt to create ribbons from carrots, yellow zucchini, or even asparagus instead of green zucchini, and the vegetable options for tossing are endless. Add steamed asparagus, green beans, peas, broccoli, or even artichoke hearts.

CURRIED CUCUMBER AND COCONUT TOSS

This salad has a surprising blend of spicy mustard seed, jalapeño, and curry that is cooled and balanced by cucumber and fresh, mature coconut meat.

YIELD: 3 SERVINGS | **TIME:** 15 MINUTES (INCLUDES PREP TIME) | **EQUIPMENT:** MEDIUM SKILLET, MEDIUM MIXING BOWL

INGREDIENTS:

2 teaspoons coconut oil

1 medium jalapeño, stem and seeds removed, and minced

½ teaspoon brown mustard seeds

1 teaspoon curry powder

½ teaspoon ground cumin

½ teaspoon sea salt

2 medium English cucumbers, diced

½ cup (40 g) grated fresh mature coconut meat

2 tablespoons (2 g) fresh cilantro leaves, minced

1 tablespoon (14 g) hemp seeds

PREPARATION:

① Heat coconut oil in a medium skillet over medium-high heat. Add jalapeño, mustard seeds, curry powder, cumin, and sea salt, and warm for 2 minutes. Set aside.

② In a medium mixing bowl, combine cucumbers, coconut, and curry sauce, and toss to coat evenly. Serve immediately topped with cilantro leaves and hemp seeds.

NOTE: If you cannot find a mature coconut, grated and dried unsweetened coconut will also work. Just soak in warm water for 20 minutes first, drain, and then incorporate into the recipe.

CREAMED ZUCCHINI SOUP

I am always looking to develop the next best creamy soup and often blend vegetables with seeds to actualize richness. After frequently making a side dish of steamed zucchini sprinkled with fresh herbs and lemon, the thought occurred to me to throw it all in the blender and see whether it would make a yummy purée. With a few additions, the experiment resulted in a brilliantly creamy and comforting zucchini soup.

YIELD: APPROXIMATELY SIX 1½-CUP (355-ML) SERVINGS | **TIME:** 20 MINUTES (INCLUDES PREP TIME) |
EQUIPMENT: VEGETABLE STEAMER, LARGE BOWL, LARGE SAUCEPAN, BLENDER

INGREDIENTS:

3 pounds (1.4 kg) zucchini, chopped (about 7 cups)

2 teaspoons (10 ml) coconut oil

1 small sweet onion, chopped

2 cloves garlic, minced

1 teaspoon fresh thyme leaves

1½ teaspoons (9 g) sea salt, plus extra for garnish

2½ cups (590 ml) water

1 tablespoon (15 ml) fresh lemon juice

½ teaspoon lemon zest

1 tablespoon (2.5 g) fresh basil, torn, plus ribbons for garnish

1 tablespoon (4 g) fresh parsley, chopped

2 teaspoons (2.6 g) fresh oregano, chopped

½ teaspoon ground black pepper

1 tablespoon (14 g) hemp seeds

PREPARATION:

① Bring water to a boil in the bottom of a vegetable steamer. Steam the zucchini in batches for 2 minutes each. Transfer to a large bowl.

② In a large saucepan over medium heat, add coconut oil and onion, and stir for 2 minutes. Add garlic and steamed zucchini and sauté for 1 minute.

③ Stir in the thyme, sea salt, water, lemon juice, lemon zest, basil, parsley, oregano, and black pepper. Heat through for 2 minutes.

④ Using a Vitamix or other high-speed blender, purée the soup in batches until smooth, about 2 minutes for each batch. Be sure to vent lid slightly and cover with a kitchen towel to avoid splatter.

⑤ Divide among bowls and top each with a few basil ribbons, a pinch of sea salt, and ½ teaspoon hemp seeds.

NOTE: If zucchini is not available, yellow squash, cauliflower, and steamed parsnips harmonize well with the blend of herbs. Also if desired, you can sweeten the soup by replacing the water with coconut water.

WEEK 3

THE BALANCED RAW BURGER

Sometimes you've just got to have a burger. To make it Balanced Raw friendly, I suggest enjoying this legume-based patty wrapped in crisp, butter leaf lettuce and topped with plenty of fresh veggies such as sprouts, cucumber, red onion, tomato, and avocado.

YIELD: 8 PATTIES | **TIME:** 30 MINUTES (INCLUDES PREP TIME) | **EQUIPMENT:** SMALL BOWL, MEDIUM SKILLET, FOOD PROCESSOR, LARGE BOWL, BAKING SHEET, GRILL

INGREDIENTS:

2 tablespoons (18 g) ground flax meal

6 tablespoons (90 ml) warm water

2 teaspoons (10 ml) coconut oil, melted, plus extra for brushing

½ cup (80 g) minced red onion

1 Serrano pepper, stem and seeds removed, and minced

2 cloves garlic, chopped

2 cups (328 g) cooked chickpeas

1 tablespoon (12 g) nutritional yeast

½ teaspoon cayenne pepper

½ teaspoon ground coriander

1 teaspoon sea salt

1 teaspoon ground cumin

½ cup (30 g) fresh parsley, chopped

2 tablespoons (12 g) fresh mint leaves, chopped

2 tablespoons (2 g) fresh cilantro leaves, chopped

¼ cup (23 g) chickpea flour

1 cup (196 g) cooked quinoa

PREPARATION:

① In a small bowl, combine flax meal and water, stir until combined, and set aside.

② Heat coconut oil in a medium skillet over medium-high heat, and add onion, pepper, and garlic, and heat for 1 minute. Set aside.

③ Combine chickpeas, nutritional yeast, cayenne pepper, coriander, sea salt, and cumin in a food processor fitted with an S blade, and pulse until combined, about 1 minute.

④ Add parsley, mint, cilantro, and flax meal mix, and pulse until well incorporated, about 30 seconds. Transfer to a large bowl and stir in onion mix and chickpea flour. Add quinoa, a little at a time, until mixed well and the dough begins to bind.

⑤ Form into 8 patties on a baking sheet. Brush both sides of patties with melted coconut oil.

⑥ Heat a grill over medium-high heat. Grill patties for 3 to 4 minutes on each side, or until lightly golden. Serve wrapped in butter leaf lettuce with desired toppings.

NOTE: If you wish to omit grilling, make a big green salad and crumble the dough over top. You can also stuff the dough into a wrap and serve with Lemon-Tahini Sauce (page 67), your favorite hummus, or Mint Chutney (page 143).

ZA'ATAR CRUSTED PARSNIP CHIPS

Za'atar is absolutely one of my favorite spice blends and ideal for pairing with sugary parsnips. These chips are savory and fiber-rich, and a welcome snack in your Balanced Raw diet.

YIELD: 12 SERVINGS | **TIME:** 10 MINUTES, PLUS 12 HOURS (INCLUDES PREP AND DEHYDRATING TIME) | **EQUIPMENT:** SPICE GRINDER, LARGE MIXING BOWL, MANDOLINE OR SHARP KNIFE, DEHYDRATOR, PARAFLEXX SHEETS

INGREDIENTS:

FOR ZA'ATAR SPICE BLEND:

¼ cup (28 g) ground sumac

3 tablespoons (13 g) dried thyme

2 tablespoons (16 g) white sesame seeds

¼ cup (12 g) dried oregano

1 teaspoon sea salt

FOR THE CHIPS:

6 medium parsnips, sliced into ⅛-inch (3-mm) disks with a mandoline or sharp knife

1 tablespoon (15 ml) fresh lemon juice

PREPARATION:

① To make the spice blind, combine sumac, thyme, sesame seeds, oregano, and sea salt in a spice grinder and pulse until thoroughly combined. Reserve 2 tablespoons (14 g) and transfer the rest to an airtight glass container and store in a dark cupboard for use within 3 months.

② To make the chips, in a large mixing bowl, combine sliced parsnips, lemon juice, and reserved 2 tablespoons (14 g) spice blend. Toss to coat evenly.

③ Turn out onto ParaFlexx sheets, ensuring slices are lying in a single layer. Dehydrate chips at 105°F (40.5°C) for 12 hours.

NOTE: You can also make this recipe using sweet potatoes or red beets, which will result in a similar flavor profile but with a more brilliant hue. If you opt to bake, do so in a 250°F (121°C) oven for 1 hour, checking every 5 to 10 minutes, and pulling those that are crispy. Turn each chip halfway through as well to ensure even baking.

WEEK 3

BODY-LOVING LEMON BARS

Lemon is refreshing any time and adds adored zing to desserts. These bars are a cinch to make and because they are rich in fresh lemon, they support detoxification and cleansing while satisfying your sweet tooth.

YIELD: APPROXIMATELY 16 ONE-BAR SERVINGS | **TIME:** 3 HOURS (INCLUDES PREP AND CHILL TIME) | **EQUIPMENT:** FOOD PROCESSOR, 8 X 8-INCH (20.3 X 20.3-CM) CAKE PAN

INGREDIENTS:

12 soft-pitted deglet noor dates

¼ cup (60 ml) water

2 cups (285 g) almond flour

2 cups (160 g) shredded unsweetened coconut

¼ cup (28 g) coconut flour

½ teaspoon sea salt

1 tablespoon (15 ml) maple syrup or agave nectar

2 teaspoons (4 g) lemon zest

6 tablespoons (90 ml) fresh lemon juice

1 tablespoon (15 ml) alcohol-free vanilla extract

¼ cup (60 ml) coconut oil, melted

PREPARATION:

① In a food processor fitted with an S blade, pulse dates with water until you achieve a chunky paste. Add almond flour, shredded coconut, coconut flour, sea salt, maple syrup or agave, lemon zest, lemon juice, and vanilla extract, and purée until combined but crumbly. Add coconut oil and mix until thoroughly incorporated, about 1 minute.

② Transfer dough to a waxed-paper-lined, 8 x 8-inch (20.3 x 20.3-cm) cake pan and using clean hands, press evenly into all edges. Freeze for at least 2½ hours, remove from pan, peel off waxed paper, and then cut into 16 bars.

NOTE: To store, wrap bars individually in waxed paper or plastic wrap and refrigerate for up to 1 week.

VAN-HEMP-NILLA BITES

Why would you ever want a dessert you cannot indulge in? I like to enjoy treats without guilt, and this one is sure to satisfy a sweet craving and at the same time deeply nourish your body. A harmonious blend of vanilla, sweet dates, coconut, and hemp seeds is pressed into ice cube trays for single-serving, anytime morsels of heaven.

YIELD: APPROXIMATELY 12 TWO-TREAT SERVINGS | **TIME:** 3 HOURS (INCLUDES PREP AND CHILL TIME) | **EQUIPMENT:** FOOD PROCESSOR, 2 STANDARD ICE CUBE TRAYS

INGREDIENTS:

20 soft-pitted deglet noor dates

½ cup (120 ml) water

1 cup (112 g) coconut flour

2 tablespoons (28 ml) maple syrup or agave nectar

¼ cup (60 ml) coconut oil, melted

2 tablespoons (28 ml) alcohol-free vanilla extract

½ teaspoon sea salt

½ cup (112 g) hemp seeds

PREPARATION:

① In a food processor fitted with an S blade, pulse dates with water until you achieve a chunky paste. Add coconut flour, maple syrup or agave, coconut oil, vanilla extract, sea salt, and hemp seeds. Pulse until well combined, about 1 minute.

② Divide and press mix into 2 greased, standard ice cube molds and freeze for at least 3 hours. Pop them out and transfer to a freezer-safe airtight container to store.

NOTE: You can make a chocolaty version by adding 2 tablespoons (16 g) raw cacao powder. If you go this route, add ¼ teaspoon cayenne pepper and ⅛ teaspoon nutmeg for a Mexican chocolate treat.

SUGAR POTATO, FIERY MUSHROOM, AND CHIPOTLE CRÈME TACOS WITH ZESTY RADISH SLAW

INGREDIENTS:

FOR THE CHIPOTLE CRÈME:

¼ cup (56 g) hemp seeds

½ cup (120 ml) water

1 tablespoon (12 g) nutritional yeast

1 tablespoon (15 ml) fresh lemon juice

¼ teaspoon sea salt

1½ teaspoons (4 g) chipotle powder

FOR THE TACOS:

1 medium sweet potato

2 teaspoons (10 ml) coconut oil

½ teaspoon ground cumin

½ teaspoon chili powder

¼ teaspoon sea salt

1 cup (70 g) chopped shiitake or oyster mushrooms (or both)

¼ cup (40 g) thinly sliced red onion

½ cup (58 g) sliced red radish

2 tablespoons (28 ml) fresh lime juice

2 tablespoons (2 g) fresh cilantro leaves, chopped, plus extra for garnish

6 non-GMO corn tortillas or 6 large butter lettuce or cabbage leaves

2 tablespoons (28 g) raw pumpkin seeds

½ medium avocado, thinly sliced

6 lime wedges

Veggie tacos have become quite a popular plant-based staple and with so many combinations of savory, spicy, and sweet ingredients available, it may have been difficult to land on a favorite, until now. The combination of crunchy and zesty radish slaw, sugary sweet potatoes, fiery mushrooms, and a smoky chipotle crème makes these tacos nearly impossible to deviate from.

YIELD: APPROXIMATELY 3 TWO-TACO SERVINGS | **TIME:** 45 MINUTES (INCLUDES PREP TIME) | **EQUIPMENT:** VEGETABLE STEAMER, 2 MEDIUM BOWLS, BLENDER, LARGE SKILLET

PREPARATION:

① To make the chipotle crème, combine hemp seeds, water, nutritional yeast, lemon juice, sea salt, and chipotle powder in a Vitamix or other high-speed blender and blend on high for 30 seconds. Set aside.

② To make the tacos, peel and dice sweet potato. Bring water to a boil in the bottom of a large vegetable steamer. Add sweet potato to basket and steam for 7 minutes. Transfer to a bowl and set aside.

③ Melt coconut oil and add to a medium mixing bowl, along with the cumin, chili powder, and sea salt. Add mushrooms and toss to coat. Let rest at room temperature until tacos are ready to assemble.

④ In a separate medium mixing bowl, combine red onion, radish, lime juice, and chopped cilantro. Toss to combine and set aside for taco assembly.

⑤ Warm tortillas in a dry skillet until pliable.

⑥ Assemble tacos by dividing sweet potatoes, mushrooms, radish slaw, pumpkin seeds, and avocado among warmed tortillas. Drizzle each with chipotle crème and top with a sprinkling of fresh cilantro. Serve each with a lime wedge.

NOTE: If you don't have chipotle powder, use 2 reconstituted dried chipotle peppers (see note on page 106 for instructions).

WEEK 3

PARSNIP RICE SUSHI WITH SWEET TAMARIND DIPPING SAUCE

Sushi is loved by so many for its stunning presentation, endless flavor combinations, and sharable bites. And the good news is that there is no need to stick to the traditional white sushi rice filling when brown rice, sweet potatoes, quinoa, cauliflower, and even parsnips work beautifully. My favorite variation is made using parsnips because they are sweet and offset the sometimes fishy essence of the nori.

YIELD: 6 SUSHI ROLLS | **TIME:** 30 MINUTES | **EQUIPMENT:** FOOD PROCESSOR, LARGE MIXING BOWL, SMALL MIXING BOWL, SUSHI ROLLING MAT, SMALL BOWL OF WARM WATER, SHARP KNIFE

INGREDIENTS:

FOR THE RICE:

3 medium parsnips, peeled and chopped, about 3 to 4 cups (330 to 440 g)

2 tablespoons (28 ml) brown rice vinegar

1 tablespoon (15 ml) water

1 teaspoon agave nectar

1 teaspoon sea salt

FOR THE TAMARIND DIPPING SAUCE:

½ cup (128 g) tamarind paste or concentrate, softened

3 tablespoons (45 ml) agave nectar

1½ tablespoons (25 ml) fresh lime juice

3 tablespoons (45 ml) coconut water

1 teaspoon coconut aminos

FOR THE ROLLS:

6 nori sheets

½ teaspoon togarashi spice powder or other chile spice blend

2 teaspoons (5.4 g) black sesame seeds

½ medium seedless cucumber, peeled and julienned

1 medium carrot, peeled and julienned

½ medium bell pepper, stem and seeds removed, and julienned

1 handful sunflower sprouts

(Continued on next page)

PARSNIP RICE SUSHI WITH SWEET
TAMARIND DIPPING SAUCE (CONTINUED)

PREPARATION:

① To prepare the rice, pulse parsnips in a food processor fitted with an S blade until mostly smooth, about 2 minutes. Transfer to a large mixing bowl and add brown rice vinegar, water, agave, and sea salt. Set aside.

② To make dipping sauce, combine tamarind paste or concentrate, agave nectar, lime juice, coconut water, and coconut aminos in a small mixing bowl. Whisk to combine and set aside.

③ To assemble the rolls, clear a space on your counter or cutting board. Lay your sushi mat down in front of you with slats running in a horizontal plane. Place the shiny side of a single sheet of nori on the mat and line up the edge of the nori with the edge of the mat closest to you.

④ Lightly wet hands, and scoop about ¾ cup (83 g) parsnip rice on the half of nori nearest you, and then using clean fingers press the rice down to completely cover the bottom two-thirds of the sheet, edge to edge horizontally. Leave a 1-inch (2.5-cm) border of nori on the edge farthest away from you.

⑤ Lightly sprinkle the rice with togarashi and black sesame seeds and then stack a couple of pieces of each vegetable and a few sprouts on top of the parsnip rice and through the centerline, leaving a bit of each vegetable hanging off the side edges for a nice presentation.

⑥ Now you are ready to roll. Place both thumbs on the underside of the mat edge closest to you. Use your thumbs to press up the mat slightly, and then gently use the four free fingers on both hands to hold the ingredients in place. Use your thumbs to roll the mat up and over the ingredients inside while still gently holding on. Do not press down and squish the rice and veggies. *Note:* Your eight fingers should roll with the mat, slightly tucking under the roll.

⑦ The mat should fully cover the roll. Using your thumb and forefinger, gently grab the edge of the mat that is on top of the roll and press back into the roll with light pressure to gently compress the insides. Pick up the exposed top mat edge with your forefinger and thumbs and roll one more time just as you did before. Give a gentle squeeze back into the roll one more time.

⑧ Peel the mat back so the roll is exposed. Dip your forefinger in warm water, and then run it along the border of exposed nori and seal the dampened nori to the roll.

⑨ Remove the mat and lay the roll on your cutting board. Using a very sharp knife and the center of the blade, saw the roll into 6 to 8 bite-size pieces. Place all pieces of the sushi on a serving dish, with the two end pieces facing up. Serve each roll with a small ramekin of Tamarind Dipping Sauce.

CHAPTER 7

WEEK 4 MAINTAIN

HOW TO LIVE BALANCED RAW EVERY DAY

THIS HAS BEEN QUITE A TRANSFORMATIVE FEW WEEKS, HASN'T IT? You scoured your kitchen; rid your pantry of junk food; shopped for and learned to store healthier ingredients; chopped, prepped, wrapped, rolled, blended, and puréed nourishing meals; detoxified your body to allow your digestive system and liver to function more efficiently; tested whether you are sensitive to common allergy-provoking foods; hopefully got plenty of rest; and learned how and why to properly include both raw and cooked foods in your diet. So what comes next? Where do you go from here? Well, you learn to live this way every day.

CERTAINLY YOU ARE AWARE OF THE HUNDREDS OF DIETS whose stated results are so appealing that they attract millions of followers every year. So often though, devoted fad dieters are only committed until the desired and promised results are not achieved, until the diets become too confining or restrictive, or quite frankly, until they feel awful because of the program's one-sided dietary approach. Some of the more provocative diets that have attracted attention include low-carb, high-protein, and even the traditional raw foods diet. What is interesting is that despite their distinct and vast differences, they all have one thing in common: each lacks balance, and balance is what keeps everything in nature living in harmony.

If you consider the Earth, which is a living organism just like you, and has unfathomable systems that operate perfectly without ever stopping, you can easily understand that its cycles and processes are balanced. One of the most critical of these is the balance between Earth and its atmosphere, which holds an appropriate balance of gases in the necessary ratio needed to sustain human beings and all living matter.

As this balance shifts because of climate change, we've experienced more extreme weather events and other natural phenomenon changes. So why should you, a living and breathing, organic being be any different? Why would you ever try to cheat balance when it is what keeps you healthy and living harmoniously?

HOW TO LIVE IN BALANCE EVERY DAY

Your body is an incredible organic machine and to maintain health and vitality, it needs a balance of macro- and micronutrients, raw and cooked foods, rest and activity, and homeostasis in hydration. Extremes in diet, exercise, supplementation, and stress will leave you weak, depleted of essential nutrients, and in a state of bodily harm. Reading to this point should have brought you closer to understanding what a Balanced Raw diet looks like, and in the five steps that follow, I will further describe how to effectively stabilize your scales so you go on living the Balanced Raw way every day.

BALANCED RAW LIFESTYLE STEP 1: ALWAYS BE CLEANSING

Does this mean you are to only drink smoothies and juices and eat only raw food the rest of your life? No. To "always be cleansing," means you adopt habits that promote daily detoxification and incorporate them into your regular routine. A few Balanced Raw favorites are listed below.

Morning liver flush: You learned in chapter 5 that adding fresh squeezed lemon juice to your morning water aids in rinsing your liver of built-up toxins from the previous day's digestive work. Make this flush a habit. All you need is the juice of half a lemon and 8 ounces (235 ml) of warm water. Drink this blend every morning before eating or enjoying any other beverage.

Night fasting: Also in chapter 5, you learned about the twelve-hour fasting period. This practice was not recommended just for your cleansing week. The twelve-hour fast between your evening meal and breakfast should become routine for you every day. This will continue to give your body the opportunity to deeply detoxify from all you ate from sunup to sundown.

Dry-brush: This is another daily cleansing ritual. Dry-brush from toe to head each day and right before showering. This action stimulates your lymph system, increases circulation, and promotes detoxification.

Avoid garbage food: An entire chapter was devoted to eliminating junk food from your pantry and your life. Continue eating clean, fresh, organic, and unprocessed foods to keep you feeling vibrant and healthy, and at your ideal weight.

Sweat every day: Whether you choose to exercise or relax in a steam room or sauna to purge your pores, detoxifying your skin via sweating is an excellent way to support your daily cleansing habit.

Move your body: So many people are simply too sedentary. A staggering percentage of the population does not move enough because of the drive to the office, a day sitting at a desk, the drive home, and hours in front of the TV. Balanced Raw living includes offsetting idleness with exercise such as walking, swimming, running, yoga, or any other physical activity or sport you enjoy. Even if you only commit to twenty minutes each day, activity stimulates blood flow and circulation, increases metabolic function, and forces you to breathe more deeply, which you learned is another supreme method of detoxification.

Skip snacking: You were encouraged in chapter 5 to avoid snacking between meals. When you allow four to five hours to pass from one meal to the next, your body begins to burn stored fat. Alternatively, when you graze throughout the day, you only burn calories from the foods eaten.

BALANCED RAW LIFESTYLE STEP 2: THRIVE WITH A HARMONIOUS BALANCE OF RAW AND COOKED FOODS

An abundance of uncooked and raw foods delivers powerful and life-giving vitamins, minerals, and enzymes to your organs and blood. The digestibility, grounding effects, and abundance of some nutrients, when met with heat, makes cooked foods an important cornerstone of your diet. You cannot consume an extreme quantity of one and not balance with the other without sacrificing tissue repair, mood stability, immunity, and efficient digestion, absorption, and elimination. You need both cooked and raw foods every day and ideally at every meal for a happy and healthy body.

To reiterate the suggestions in chapter 1, the Balanced Raw diet contains at least 50 percent raw foods, with the rest coming from cooked or fermented fare. Depending on your lifestyle, preferences, and the changing seasons, your raw intake may be higher. According to Joel Fuhrman, M.D., an expert in nutritional medicine, filling at least half of your plate with nutrient-dense raw fruits and vegetables, and the other with cooked foods such as grains, legumes, roots, and greens and other nutrient-rich foods such as seeds and sea vegetables, supports a healthy and balanced diet and is one of the greatest secrets to optimum health.

BALANCED RAW LIFESTYLE STEP 3: DRINK WATER ALL DAY EVERY DAY

Do you ever get a headache that comes out of nowhere or achy muscles when you did not work out? How about feelings of general malaise or sensitivity to cold? Did you know that in many cases, these uncomfortable sensations in your body are alarms sounding to announce you are dehydrated?

No lie. Dehydration is a chronic disorder suffered by millions of people, and a serious one at that. You can survive for up to a month without food, but beyond three or four days, if you do not have water, your body will shut down and turn off. Let me share with you some ways water supports your body.

Digestion: You learned in chapter 5 about waste removal. Can you guess what your most effective delivery system to remove this toxic waste is? You got it. Water. During digestive processes, water delivers nutrients and toxins to your bloodstream and organs for either filtration or absorption and then excretes the waste through urine and feces. On average, you lose between $1\frac{1}{2}$ to 2 quarts (1.4 to 1.9 L) of water each day in your urine. That equates to between 6 and 8 cups! Think about this for a minute. When you are dehydrated, your body has very little water left after excretion, and this water is usually concentrated with remaining toxins. Without new water to continue flushing your system, this toxic water keeps getting filtered back through your organs, brain, and tissues. Yuck!

Brain function: Your complex brain is composed of between 80 and 90 percent water. Sounds unreal, doesn't it? All of your thoughts, memories, emotions, and creativity take place in a pool of water. So you need to nourish your brain with clean water throughout the day to keep your thoughts clear, headaches at bay, memory sharp, and creativity flowing. Without enough H_2O, you can become easily distracted, may be unable to recall short- and long-term memories, may experience brain fog, and will certainly experience headaches.

Kidney and bladder health: Have you ever experienced the excruciating and debilitating discomfort of a urinary tract or kidney infection? If so, you know both are incredibly unpleasant and, in most cases, can be avoided with adequate consumption of filtered water. Every day, your kidneys are tasked with filtering waste particles. Drinking clean, filtered water throughout the day keeps them flushed and working optimally. Also, with increased water consumption, you will likely be urinating more frequently, which is a good thing, but do your best not to hold it. Doing so traps bacteria-infested water in your urinary tract and can cause infections and bladder discomfort.

Breathing support: This may come as a surprise, but you lose 2 to 4 cups (475 to 950 ml) of water each day just through breathing. Your lungs require water to take in oxygen and release carbon dioxide efficiently, and you need to be aptly hydrated for respiratory health. Sometimes just an increase in water consumption will lesson symptoms of respiratory conditions such as asthma and allergies!

Muscle and joint lubrication: If your muscles or joints feel achy, it could be due to an illness coming on, post-workout soreness, or in many cases, dehydration. Your muscles are 75 percent water, and when organ tissues and blood are in need of hydration, they can rob water from your muscles, resulting in unexplained aches and tightness.

Cardiovascular health: Your heart is made of nearly 75 percent water, and staying hydrated supports cardio-vascular activity and healthy circulation. Water is also essential for regulating blood pressure and body tempera-ture, so if you are sensitive to cold or are feeling numbness or tingling in your extremities, it may be due to dehydration.

Water—the Best Sources, How Much You Need, and When to Take It In

You have likely heard that you need anywhere from six to eight glasses of water per day, to half your weight in ounces, to the magic number of 64 ounces (1.9 L) daily. There is enough research now that suggests drinking half your weight in ounces is sufficient for the average and sed-entary person. If you are active and involved in exercise where a great deal of perspiration is excreted, you need to supplement with at least 24 ounces (710 ml) of water for every hour of exertion, and even more if you are practicing hot yoga or working out in hot weather. If you are involved in vigorous exercise outside in the summer months, you can lose up to 2 or even 3 quarts (liters) of water in an hour just through sweat!

To Filter or Not to Filter?

Hands down, no questions asked, filter your water, because bottled water is known to be just as harmful as water straight from the tap. According to the National Resources Defense Council, this is because water-bottling regula-tions are not stringent enough. Regarding tap water, the nonprofit Environmental Working Group (EWG) in 2005 sampled the water supply in forty-two states and discov-ered that it contained 260 contaminants. However, the Environmental Protection Agency (EPA) regulates only ninety-one of these, with sixty contaminants commonly found throughout the country, including asbestos, arsenic, cadmium, *E. coli*, pesticides, hormones from birth control pills, antibiotics, uranium, herbicides, fluoride, lead, para-sites, and traces of antidepressants and other medications. Definitely not anything you want to be ingesting on a regu-lar basis—or ever, for that matter.

Invest in a home filter that removes the most common and harmful contaminants. Filtering your shower water is just as important, because your skin absorbs even more of the contaminants from unfiltered water than you absorb through your mouth, so be sure to get a filter for your showerhead, too.

There is no true comparable substitute for clean, fresh water. Even nourishing drinks including herbal tea and fruit and vegetable juices must first be metabolized, making them inferior to water, which gets right into your bloodstream, tissues, and organs without having to go through any other processes.

Caffeinated beverages, alcohol, and carbonated drinks rob your organs, tissues, and skin of hydration, so you will need to drink 1 to 3 cups (235 to 705 ml) of water for every one of these other liquids just to neutralize their dehydrating effects.

One of the first ways to monitor your level of hydration is by how energized you are. Often when you are feeling listless, you need to drink more water. Also consider your level of concentration, focus, and mood, and whether or not you have a dull headache. If you are experiencing any of the negative effects, drink up and monitor how you feel after. Also look at the color of your urine. If you are hydrated, your urine should be clear. If you are teetering on dehydration, your urine will look like lemonade, and if severely dehydrated it will be dark yellow or even orange.

Throughout the day, be sure to drink the majority of your water between meals, and before, during, and after exercise. Prior to any meal, leave a water-free window of twenty to thirty minutes to avoid dilution of digestive juices. I also suggest not drinking more than 8 ounces (235 ml) of water before bed because too much can disrupt sleep by making you have to get up to use the bathroom in the middle of the night.

Also remember, feeling thirsty is a sign of dehydration, not just a desire for liquid refreshment. If you are thirsty, you have dipped well below optimal hydration levels. To avoid the health trap of chronic dehydration, follow these recommendations and drink water to feel alive!

BALANCED RAW LIFESTYLE STEP 4: WITH A FEW EXCEPTIONS, NUTRIENTS SHOULD COME FROM REAL FOOD AND NOT CAPSULES

There are so many supplements out there and so much confusion surrounding the topic. Why did we all start taking supplements in the first place? For one, now more than ever, there is nutrient scarcity in our food because of pesticide use, the practice of genetically modifying food, crops being repeatedly grown on the same soil, which, over time, loses its nutrient density, and longer food delivery times. By the time food reaches you, unless purchased locally, it has been losing the strength of its nutrients from spending days on truck beds and grocery store shelves.

To rectify this issue and ensure ample intake of vitamins and minerals, supplements made their way into our mainstream diet. In addition, food toxins are at an all-time high and we burden our bodies with excessive stress, lack of sleep, and exposure to environmental free radicals, all of which demand some kind of diet supplementation. And

WHEN AN ALARMING COLOR OF URINE IS NO CAUSE FOR CONCERN

You may experience a few instances when the color of your urine appears alarming but is actually no cause for concern. You may note a pink or rosy hue, for example, if you have recently consumed beets, dark orange urine if you just had a B_{12} injection or took a sublingual tablet, or very bright yellow urine if you have just eaten asparagus.

last, billions of dollars are spent each year on advertisements to get you to buy supplements of all kinds.

Taking all this into consideration, it should be no surprise if you have a cupboard that resembles an apothecary. But do you really need all those bottles? Is the money you pay for these tablets ill spent? Are you confused about which ones to take with food and which require an empty stomach? Do you ever wonder whether they are counteracting each other, making them pointless to take? The lack of understanding can leave you taking supplements you do not need, or if you have given up on the idea out of sheer frustration, you may be avoiding some supplements that could genuinely support your health.

Enjoying a plant-based and organic foods diet, preparing meals at home, drinking plenty of filtered water, exercising, reducing stress, getting plenty of rest, and regularly detoxing your body are your most reliable lines of defense against disease. When you are living the Balanced Raw way, you need not inundate your medicine cabinet with an entourage of supplements. This is not to say all supplements are unnecessary, and there are certainly special circumstances that require a more robust supplementation regimen. But for those of you who have been following a raw, vegan, or vegetarian diet for some time, or have mild symptoms of fatigue, sleeplessness, muscle aches, or general feelings of malaise, there are a few supplements I believe are very supportive to Balanced Raw living and to the reduction of these symptoms. Here are my top four recommendations:

Vitamin D₃: For years, magazines, doctors, radio, and television have advised us to stay out of the sun to protect ourselves from skin cancer. Yet now we hear that many of us are grossly deficient in vitamin D. The irony here is the ultraviolet rays of the sun are what provide you with naturally occurring and highly absorbable vitamin D.

Vitamin D is synthesized when these rays strike your skin, so sun scare tactics have effectively kept you from being exposed and unable to absorb this necessary nutrient unless you do so with supplementation.

The most efficient way to get your daily dose is to spend twenty minutes outside during the middle of the day when the sun is high. But if you are at work like most of the world during those hours, taking a vitamin D₃ supplement instead of catching some rays is your next best solution.

For healthy bones, it is not a calcium tablet you need, but rather vitamin D₃ along with an abundance of calcium-rich dark leafy greens and legumes. Vitamin D₃ is what helps your body absorb the bioavailable calcium from these foods. Vitamin D₃ is also responsible for neuromuscular health and immunity, and reduces inflammation. Studies indicate the required daily minimum (for adults) of this essential nutrient is 5,000 IU. Also note, vitamin D₃ is fat-soluble and must be taken with a serving of fat-strong food such as avocado, or flax or chia seeds to ensure efficient absorption.

Vitamin B₁₂: You may be deficient in this vitamin, especially if you have been following a strict vegetarian or vegan diet, because it is mostly present in animal foods. Signs of deficiency may include lack of energy, brain fog, muscle aches and fatigue, chronic infections, diarrhea, constipation, or weight loss. The recommended minimum of highly absorbable vitamin B₁₂ is 4 to 7 mcg daily for adults. To absorb that much, you are advised to take at least 250 mcg of methylcobalamin B₁₂ daily in the form of a sublingual tablet or 2,000 to 2,500 mcg in a weekly injection. Don't be frightened; the shot is quick, and the profound energy and enhanced body functions you will experience are worth the momentary discomfort.

It is also not a bad idea to supplement your intake with B_{12}-containing plant foods, such as spirulina and nutritional yeast (if fortified with B_{12}), but do not rely on these for your daily requirements, because 1 tablespoon (8 g) of spirulina has only 4 mcg. A lack of B_{12} is not to be overlooked, because it is required for so many vital functions, including protein and red blood cell synthesis, nerve and brain function, energy, metabolic functions, and immunity.

Magnesium: Magnesium participates in more than three hundred functions in your body, yet is unfortunately one of the minerals you might very well be deficient in. Unless you are eating organic plant foods grown in naturally composted soil, you are likely not getting adequate levels. In addition, the consumption of processed food also depletes your body of magnesium. And your body's ability to absorb it can be reduced by environmental factors such as stress, caffeine, chemicals, medications, and alcohol. Common side effects of magnesium deficiency include headaches, insomnia, anxiety, muscle soreness, high blood pressure, and constipation.

A minimum of 300 mg of elemental magnesium per day is the recommended adult daily allowance. Chelated versions such as magnesium glycinate and taurate are the most highly absorbable types. To ensure an adequate intake, take a chelated oral supplement in the morning and on an empty stomach, and also eat plenty of organic and magnesium-rich foods such as black beans, buckwheat flour, artichokes, pumpkin seeds, raw cacao, and cooked spinach.

Probiotics: Did you know the majority of your immune system is located in your belly? And do you know what is essential for the health of your immune system? Bacteria, especially beneficial bacteria. Unfortunately, your good gut bugs are depleted by the use of antibiotics, preservatives, additives, and pesticides in food, and from an excess of sugar and alcohol.

To rebuild a strong gut army, you need a consistent dose of quality probiotics. Probiotics are strains of beneficial living bacteria. They keep disease-promoting organisms, such as candida, parasites, and food-borne pathogens, from winning the war and keep you feeling your best. Not only do they support immune function, but they also ward off infection and protect against digestive distress. It is not unusual for someone first taking a probiotic to have more regular bowel movements, a reduction in allergies and food sensitivities, and less digestive discomforts such as gas, bloating, constipation, and diarrhea.

If you are not already taking a probiotic, get one that is dairy-free and has multiple strains and colony-forming units, or CFUs, well into the billions. It is also healthful to ensure the one you select contains *Bacillus coagulans* or *Lactobacillus*. Take the capsules right away, and then make a regular habit of taking them twice per day and with meals to encourage adequate absorption.

BALANCED RAW LIFESTYLE STEP 5: LET THE RECIPES BE A SOURCE FOR INSPIRATION

You could absolutely make a habit of living a Balanced Raw lifestyle by adhering to the meal schedule in week 3, because the dishes are not only delectable, but they also provide you with a promising balance of raw and cooked foods, phytonutrients, and macronutrients. If you fell in love with the recommended smoothies and juices, feel free to join the liquid breakfast club and continue blending your morning meal. There is no harm in doing so, and you will get a nice jolt of nutrient energy to start your day.

A day of Balanced Raw eating may look like this: your meals will include a balance of fat, protein, and carbohydrates, and both raw and cooked foods. The only exception is breakfast because you may choose to enjoy a raw smoothie or juice. Outlined below is an example of a Balanced Raw meal plan.

Breakfast: A blended beverage such as the **Blue Greens Smoothie**, or a **Veggie Blast Fresh Pressed Juice**, or a serving of the **Pumpkin Spice Morning Chia Porridge** if you prefer a heartier morning meal.

Lunch: Raw soup such as the **Hot Hot Pepper and Tomato Soup** and a serving of grain salad such as the **Fiesta Millet Salad with Smoky Avocado Cream.**

Dinner: A light meal including both cooked and raw food such as the **Citrus, Pomegranate, and Celeriac Salad** and a cup of the **Glowing Greens and Hemp Soup**. Enjoy a treat with dinner if you choose, such as the **Body-Loving Lemon Bars.**

My hope is the recipes shared throughout this book will inspire you to experiment with the abundance of food options available to you. I encourage you to explore and search for other dishes that support your Balanced Raw diet and to build a library of recipes that can be referred to often. As you regularly prepare Balanced Raw cuisine and practice the recommendations made in this chapter, you will grow accustomed to living this way and form new habits for health, and it won't be long until you are a Balanced Raw pro.

I wish you joy on your journey to wellness and encourage you to thank yourself for making a commitment to Balanced Raw living. You have already accomplished so much by reading this book and putting the principles to the test in order to restore and rebalance. As you continue to nurture your body, mind, and spirit, may you feel more nourished, balanced, and whole, and achieve the optimum health and vitality you deserve.

RESOURCES

FOOD RETAILERS

Chickpea miso
www.great-eastern-sun.com

Coconut aminos and sugar
www.coconutsecret.com

Organic gluten-free grains and flour
www.arrowheadmills.com

Organic local produce
www.localharvest.org

Organic spices
www.mountainroseherbs.com

Probiotics, vitamins, and minerals
www.megafood.com

Sprouts and sprouting kits
www.sproutpeople.org

Superfoods
www.sunfood.com

KITCHEN ITEMS

Centrifuge juicer
www.breville.com

Excalibur dehydrator and drying sheets
www.sunfood.com

High-speed blender
www.vitamix.com

Masticating juicer
www.sunfood.com

Nontoxic cookware
www.ceramcor.com

Water filters
www.multipure.com

SUPPORTIVE WEBSITES

Be Well Buzz
www.bewellbuzz.com

Care2 Community
www.care2.com

Dr. Joseph Mercola
www.mercola.com

Forks Over Knives
www.forksoverknives.com

HappyCow vegetarian food finder
www.happycow.com

Haute Health (author's site)
www.hautehealthnow.com

Institute for Integrative Nutrition
www.integrativenutrition.com

Josh Blatter Yoga
www.joshblatteryoga.com

Natural News
www.naturalnews.com

VegNews
www.vegnews.com

Yoga Journal
www.yogajournal.com

NOTES

PART 1: ADOPTING THE BALANCED RAW LIFESTYLE

CHAPTER 1

• Neal Barnard, M.D., and Gabriel Cousens, M.D., on diabetes and veganism. "A Cure for Diabetes through Veganism," YouTube, www.youtube.com/watch?v=0viz3jej1w0, uploaded August 1, 2008.

• The Cancer Project, "The Five Worst Foods to Grill," www.cancerproject.org/media/news/fiveworstfoodsreport.php, viewed July 2012.

• Karen Collins, R.D. "To Grill or Not to Grill—Take Steps to Minimize Cancer Risk," MSNBC, www.msnbc.msn.com/id/8499202/ns/health-diet_and_nutrition/t/grill-or-not-grill/#.T_XflHB1Efo, created July 8, 2005.

• Caldwell B. Esselstyn, Jr., M.D., on the health benefits of avoiding oils. "No Oil—Not Even Olive Oil!" YouTube, www.youtube.com/watch?v=b_o4YBQPKtQ, uploaded September 9, 2011.

• Caldwell B. Esselstyn, Jr., M.D., on treating heart disease. "Prevent and Reverse Heart Disease," www.heartattackproof.com/qanda.htm, viewed August 2012.

• Joel Fuhrman, M.D., on raw versus cooked foods. "Raw vs. Cooked?" www.drfuhrman.com/faq/question.aspx?sid=16&qindex=4, created and updated 2004–2012.

• Maria Lopez-Jurado, et al. "Evaluation of Zinc and Magnesium Bioavailability from Pea Sprouts—Effect of Illumination and Different Germination Periods," *International Journal of Food Science & Technology*, pp. 618–626, created 2006.

• Ann MacDonald, editor, *Harvard Health Publications*, Harvard Medical School, on stretch receptors in the stomach. "Why Eating Slowly May Help You Feel Full Faster," www.health.harvard.edu/blog/why-eating-slowly-may-help-you-feel-full-faster-20101019605, viewed October 19, 2012.

• Joseph Mercola, D.O., on coconut oil. "Here's the Smarter Oil Alternative I Recommend to Replace Those Other Oils in Your Kitchen," mercola.com, products.mercola.com/coconut-oil, viewed March 2012.

• Joseph Mercola, D.O., on creating acrylamide when heating foods. "When You Heat Natural Plant-Based Foods You Can Get Cancer-Causing Acrylamide," articles.mercola.com/sites/articles/archive/2012/06/09/when-you-heat-natural-plantbased-foods-you-can-get-acrylamide-and-cancer.aspx#_edn8, viewed June 9, 2012.

• Frederic Patenaude, raw food author and expert, on high-fat content in raw food diets. "Fats in the Raw Foods Diet," www.fredericpatenaude.com/questions/fat.html, viewed July 2012.

• Purdue University, Animal Sciences, on best foods to grill. "Meat Quality and Safety," ag.ansc.purdue.edu/meat_quality/grilling.html, created June 2, 2000.

• Tracey Roizman, D.C., on hunger signals. "How Does Your Stomach Tell Your Brain That You're Full?" Livestrong, www.livestrong.com/article/489875-how-does-your-stomach-tell-your-brain-that-youre-full, viewed June 11, 2012.

• Ray Sahelian, M.D., on the health benefits and nutrition of grapes. www.raysahelian.com/grape.html, viewed May 20, 2012.

• University of Maryland Medical Center, on health benefits of omega-3 fatty acids. "Omega-3 Fatty Acids Overview," www.umm.edu/altmed/articles/omega-3-000316.htm, viewed June 2012.

• University of Maryland Medical Center, on health benefits of omega-6 fatty acids. "Omega-6 Fatty Acids Overview," www.umm.edu/altmed/articles/omega-6-000317.htm, viewed June 2012.

CHAPTER 2

• George Mateljan Foundation. "Health Benefits of Buckwheat," WHFoods, www.whfoods.com/genpage.php?tname=foodspice&dbid=11, viewed August 2012.

• Joel Fuhrman, M.D., on human protein requirements. "Food Scoring Guide—Complete Protein," Disease Proof, the official blog of Joel Fuhrman, www.diseaseproof.com/archives/2008/01/articles/diet-myths, created January 31, 2008.

• John McDougall, M.D., on plant foods as a protein source. "Plant Foods Have a Complete Amino Acid Composition," American Heart Association, circ.ahajournals.org/content/105/25/e197.full, viewed September 2012.

• Dean M. Ornish, M.D., on fat intake. "A Diet That Restricts Daily Fat Intake to 10 Percent Can Help in the Fight Against Heart Disease," Heart Information Network, dwb.unl.edu/Teacher/NSF/C11/C11Links/www.heartinfo.com/diet10orn3497.htm, created and updated 1996–2000.

• Alvin Powell, *Harvard Health Publications*, Harvard University, on diabetes. "Obesity? Diabetes? We've Been Set Up," news.harvard.edu/gazette/story/2012/03/the-big-setup, created March 7, 2012.

• World Health Organization, Food and Agriculture Organization, United Nations University, *Humans and Protein Needs*, WHO technical report series 935, created 2007.

PART 2: THE BALANCED RAW SYSTEM

CHAPTER 4

• Adam Abraham, founder of "Talk for Food" Radio, on genetically modified foods. "Talk for Food—Genetically Engineered Hijacking of American Health," podcast, created July 2012.

• Mike Adams, editor, www.NaturalNews.com, "Baked goods sold in U.S.A. contain potassium bromate, a carcinogen banned in Europe but allowed in the U.S. due to chemical loophole," from 25 Amazing Facts About Food, www.naturalnews.com/035542_potassium_bromate_baked_goods_cancer.html, created April 12, 2012.

• Nicole M. Avena, Ph.D., Pedro Rada, M.D., and Bartley G. Hoebel, Ph.D., on causes of sugar addiction. "Evidence for Sugar Addiction," U.S. Library of Medicine, www.ncbi.nlm.nih.gov/pubmed/17617461, created May 18, 2007.

• Nicholas Bakalar. "Nutrition: MSG Use Linked to Obesity," *New York Times*, www.nytimes.com/2008/08/26/health/nutrition/26nutr.html, created August 25, 2008.

• Sherry Baker, health sciences editor. "Nitrates and Nitrites May Cause Alzheimer's, Diabetes, and Parkinson's Disease," *Natural News*, www.naturalnews.com/026566_nitrates_disease_diabetes.html, created July 7, 2009.

• Russell L. Blaylock, M.D. "The Connection Between Multiple Sclerosis and Aspartame," Truth in Labeling, www.truthinlabeling.org/Blaylock-Aspartame-AndMultipleSclerosis-Neurosurgeon's Warning.html, created February 26, 2006.

• Mark Borigini, M.D., on gluten sensitivity. "Gluten Sensitivity—Nonsense or New Disease?" *Psychology Today*, www.psychologytoday.com/blog/overcoming-pain/201203gluten-sensitivity-nonsense-or-new-disease, created March 25, 2012.

• Matt Brignall, N.D. "Hydrogenated Oils and Trans Fats," WebMD, http://blogs.webmd.com/integrative-medicine-wellness/2007/08/hydrogenated-oils-and-trans-fats.html, created August 20, 2007.

• T. Colin Campbell, Ph.D., and Thomas M. Campbell II, M.D. *The China Study: Startling Implication for Diet, Weight Loss, and Long-Term Health*, Dallas: Benbella Books, 2006.

• Candice Choi. "Coke, Pepsi Make Changes to Caramel Coloring to Avoid Cancer Warning," Huffington Post, www.huffingtonpost.com/2012/03/08/coke-pepsi-cancer-warning-caramel-coloring-changes_n_1333074.html, created March 8, 2012.

• Kayla T. Daniel, Ph.D. "The Whole Soy Story," Clinical Rounds—Designs for Health Teleconferences, podcast, created June 17, 2009.

• Christine H. Farlow, D.C. "Do You Eat Foods with Any of These 9 Cancer-Causing Chemicals?" *Healthy Eating Advisor*, www.healthyeatingadvisor.com/9cancer-causingchemicals.html, created and updated 2004–2009.

• Bruce Fife, N.D. *The Detox Book: How to Detoxify Your Body to Improve Your Health, Stop Disease, and Reverse Aging*, revised second edition. Colorado Springs, CO: Piccadilly Books, 2001.

• Burton Goldberg, author of *Alternative Medicine: The Definitive Guide*, on acidity and disease. "Acid-Alkaline Balance and Its Importance to Your Health," Burton-Goldberg.com, www.burtongoldberg.com/page84.html, viewed November 10, 2012.

• Michael I. Goran, Ph.D., Emily A. Ventura, Ph.D., and Stanley J. Ulljaszek, Ph.D. "High Fructose Corn Syrup and Diabetes Prevalence: A Global Perspective," *Global Public Health: An International Journal for Research, Policy and Practice*, www.scribd.com/doc/114642754/Global-Public-Health, published May 1, 2012.

• James M. Greenblatt, M.D. "Is Gluten Making You Depressed?" *Psychology Today*, www.psychologytoday.com/blog/the-breakthrough-depression-solution/201105/is-gluten-making-you-depressed, created May 24, 2011.

• Gardiner Harris. "FDA Panel to Consider Warnings for Artificial Food Colorings," *New York Times*, www.nytimes.com/2011/03/30/health/policy/30fda.html?_r=1, created March 29, 2011.

• Jane Higdon, Ph.D. *An Evidence-Based Approach to Dietary Phytochemicals*. New York, NY: Thieme Medical Publishers, 2007.

• Carol Hoernlein, P.E. "Health Implications of MSG," MSG Truth, www.msgtruth.org, created April 12, 2012.

• International Food Information Council and U.S. Food and Drug Administration. "Food Ingredients and Colors," www.fda.gov/downloads/Food/FoodIngredientsPackaging/ucm094249.pdf, updated May 23, 2011.

• Rachel Johnson, Ph.D., M.P.H., R.D. "Six Surprising Sources of Sugar," *Eating Well*, www.eatingwell.com/blogs/health_blog/6_surprising_sources_of_sugar, created January 26, 2012.

• Sage Kalmus, C.H.H.C., on diglycerides. "What Is Bad about Mono- and Diglycerides?" Livestrong, www.livestrong.com/article/445850-what-is-bad-about-mono-diglycerides, created May 19, 2011.

• O. Lee, et al. "Fructose Contributes to the Development of Obesity and Fatty Liver," Green Med Info, www.greenmedinfo.com/article/fructose-contributes-development-obesity-and-fatty-live, created March 16, 2009.

• James T. C. Li, M.D., Ph.D. "Food Intolerance vs. Food Allergy—What's the Difference?" Mayo Clinic, www.mayoclinic.com/health/food-allergy/AN01109, created June 3, 2011.

• Joseph Mercola, D.O. "First Ever Lifetime Feeding Study Finds Genetically Engineered Corn Causes Massive Tumors, Organ Damage, and Early Death," articles.mercola.com/sites/articles/archive/2012/09/22/superbugs-destruct-food-supply.aspx, created September 22, 2012.

• Joseph Mercola, D.O., on coconut oil. "Here's the Smarter Oil Alternative I Recommend to Replace Those Other Oils in Your Kitchen," Mercola.com, products.mercola.com/coconut-oil, created March 2012.

• Andreas Moritz, H.H.P. "The Link Between Processed Food and Weight Gain Is the Liver," Ezine Articles, www.ezinearticles.com/6459822, created 2011.

• Alpad Pusztai, Ph.D., and S. W. B. Ewen, M.D. "Health Hazards of Genetically Manipulated Food," Soy Info, www.soyinfo.com/haz/gehaz.shtml, created September 26, 1999.

• Lisa Richards, founder, TheCandidaDiet.com. "Candida Diet—Foods to Avoid," www.thecandidadiet.com/foodstoavoid.htm, created July 2012.

• Jeffrey M. Smith, author of *Seeds of Deception*, on genetically modified organisms (GMOs). "Healthy Living Starts with Avoiding GMOs, Monsanto, and More," podcast, created July 2012.

• Dani Veracity. "The Hidden Dangers of Caffeine—How Coffee Causes Exhaustion, Fatigue, and Addiction," *Natural News*, www.naturalnews.com/012352_caffeine_coffee.html, created October 11, 2005.

• Cathy Wong, N.D., C.N.S. "Candida Diet—a List of Foods to Avoid Entirely," About.com, altmedicine.about.com/od/popularhealthdiets/a/candida_foods1.htm, created September 27, 2011.

• Robert Young, Ph.D. "Overacidity and Overgrowth of Yeast, Fungus, and Mold," Consumer Health Organization of Canada, www.consumerhealth.org/articles/display.cfm?ID=19990303223214, created July 2012.

CHAPTER 5

• Jason Boehm, C.N.S., M.M.C. "Why Juice Cleanses Can Make You Feel Bad," PEER-trainer.com, www.peertrainer.com/cleanse/why_juice_and_master_cleanses_make_you_feel_bad.aspx, created January 4, 2012.

• John Douillard, M.D. *Perfect Health for Kids: Ten Ayurvedic Health Secrets Every Parent Must Know*. Berkeley, CA: North Atlantic Books, 2003.

• Jean-Jacques Dugoua, Ph.D. "Milk Thistle for Liver Damage," Healthier Talk, www.healthiertalk.com/milk-thistle-liver-damage-0800, created August 26, 2009.

• Alejandro Junger, M.D. "The Clean Diet Basics," EveryDiet.org, www.everydiet.org/diet/clean-diet, viewed July 2012.

• National Institutes of Health. "What Is B6 and What Does It Do?" ods.od.nih.gov/factsheets/VitaminB6-QuickFacts, viewed October 7, 2012.

• Sharon Thiel, R.M.T., C.Y.T. "What Vitamins Help Maintain a Healthy Liver?" Livestrong, www.livestrong.com/article/284043-what-vitamins-help-maintain-a-healthy-liver, viewed October 19, 2012.

• Andrew Weil, M.D. "Vitamin Library—Probiotics," www.drweil.com/drw/u/ART03052/Probiotics.html, viewed November 19, 2012.

CHAPTER 6

• T. Colin Campbell, Ph.D., and Thomas M. Campbell II, M.D. *The China Study: Startling Implication for Diet, Weight Loss, and Long-Term Health*. Dallas: Benbella Books, 2006.

• Katherine Kam and Louise Chang, M.D. "Going Gluten-Free—What to Know about Celiac Disease, Gluten Sensitivity, and Gluten-Free Diets," WebMD, www.webmd.com/digestive-disorders/celiac-disease/features/gluten-intolerance-against-grain, created February 16, 2012.

• Stanley F. Wainapel, M.D., M.P.H., and Avital Fast, M.D. *Food Intolerance—Alternative Medicine and Rehabilitation*, Demos Medical, published 2003, www.ncbi.nlm.nih.gov/books/NBK11244.

• WebMD. "Symptoms of Lactose Intolerance," www.webmd.com/digestive-disorders/tc/lactose-intolerance-symptoms, created July 19, 2011.

CHAPTER 7

• Nikolaos Alexopoulos, M.D., Charalambos Vlachopoulos, M.D., and Christodoulos Stefanadis, M.D. "Effect of Dark Chocolate on Arterial Function in Healthy Individuals," National Center for Biotechnology Information, www.ncbi.nlm.nih.gov/pubmed/15925737?itool=EntrezSystem2.PEntrez.Pubmed.Pubmed_ResultsPanel.Pubmed_RVDocSum&ordinalpos=7, created June 18, 2005.

• Gale Bernhardt, coach, USA Triathlon Team, on sweating and proper hydration. "Cracking the Code on Sweat Rates," Active.com, www.active.com/triathlon/Articles/Cracking-the-Code-on-Sweat-Rates, viewed September 2012.

• H.S. Brown, Ph.D., D.R. Bishop, M.P.H., and C.A. Rowan, M.S.P.H. "The Toxic Effect of Chlorine Skin Absorption," Purify My Water, www.purifymywater.com/article2.pdf, viewed September 15, 2012.

• Charles Duhigg. "Millions in U.S. Drink Contaminated Water, Records Show," *New York Times*, www.nytimes.com/2009/12/08/business/energy-environment/08water.html?pagewanted=all, created December 7, 2009.

• Charles Duhigg. "U.S. Bolsters Chemical Restrictions for Water," *New York Times*, www.nytimes.com/2010/03/23/business/23water.html?_r=1, created March 22, 2010.

• Environmental Working Group. "Over 300 Pollutants in U.S. Tap Water," About.com, environment.about.com/gi/o.htm?zi=1/XJ&zTi=1&sdn=environment&cdn=newsissues&tm=11&f=20&su=p284.13.342.ip_p504.6.342.ip_&tt=2&bt=0&bts=0&st=37&zu=http%3A//www.ewg.org/tapwater/yourwater/index.php, created December 2009.

• Alison Evert, M.S., R.D., C.D.E. "Magnesium in Diet," Medline Plus, www.nlm.nih.gov/medlineplus/ency/article/002423.htm, created March 2, 2011.

• Joel Fuhrman, M.D., on raw versus cooked food. "Raw vs. Cooked?" www.drfuhrman.com/faq/question.aspx?sid=16&qindex=4, viewed July 2012.

• Varnada Karriem-Norwood, M.D. "Vitamin B12 Deficiency: Causes, Symptoms, and Treatment," WebMD, www.webmd.com/food-recipes/guide/vitamin-b12-deficiency-symptoms-causes, viewed April 18, 2012.

• Ashley Koff, R.D. "Three Ways to Improve Your Body's Metabolic Burn," Dr. Oz, www.doctoroz.com/videos/3-ways-improve-metabolic-burn, created February 15, 2012.

• MayoClinic.com. "Symptoms of Dehydration," www.mayoclinic.com/health/dehydration/DS00561/DSECTION=symptoms, created January 7, 2011.

• John McDougall, M.D., on the health implications of fats. "Truth about Fat," DrMcDougall.com, goodveg.squidoo.com/columns/vegalicious/truth-about-fat, viewed October 17, 2012.

• Joseph Mercola, D.O. "Health Benefits of B12," Mercola.com, products.mercola.com/vitamin-b12-spray, created September 2012.

• Joseph Mercola, D.O. "How Much Vitamin D Do You Really Need to Take?" Mercola.com, articles.mercola.com/sites/articles/archive/2009/10/10/vitamin-d-experts-reveal-the-truth.aspx, created October 10, 2009.

• Joseph Mercola, D.O. "Intermittent Fasting Benefits," Mercola.com, fitness.mercola.com/sites/fitness/archive/2012/09/14/intermittent-fasting-benefits.aspx, created September 14, 2012.

• Joseph Mercola, D.O., and David Wolfe, on processed foods and illness. "David Wolfe Interview—Why Do People Really Get Sick?" Mercola.com, articles.mercola.com/sites/articles/archive/2010/02/13/david-wolfe-interview.aspx, created February 13, 2010.

• Monica Myklebust, M.D., and Jenna Wunder, M.P.H., R.D. "Healing Foods Pyramid—Water," University of Michigan Health System, www.med.umich.edu/umim/food-pyramid/water.htm, created 2010.

• Jack Norris, R.D. "Are You Getting Enough B12 from Your Vegan Diet?" Roohit.com, roohit.com/site/showArc.php?shid=b81ee, created September 2012.

• NSF Consumer Information. "Lead in Drinking Water," www.nsf.org/consumer/newsroom/fact_water_lead.asp?program=WaterTre, viewed September 14, 2012.

• NSF International. *Pharmaceuticals in Drinking Water Guide*, www.nsf.org/consumer/newsroom/pdf/pharmaceuticals_water.pdf, viewed September 14, 2012.

• Nutrition Ecology International Center. "Panel 5—Milk and Dairy in Human Nutrition," www.nutritionecology.org/panel5/intro.html, viewed November 3, 2012.

• Office of Dietary Supplements. "Vitamin D Fact Sheet," ods.od.nih.gov/factsheets/VitaminD-HealthProfessional, created 2010.

• Eric D. Olson, on tap versus bottled water. "Pure Drink or Pure Hype?" Natural Resources Defense Council, www.nrdc.org/water/drinking/bw/chap4.asp, created April 1999.

• Michael B. Schachter, M.D., P.C. "The Importance of Magnesium to Human Nutrition," Schachter Center for Complementary Medicine, www.mbschachter.com/importance_of_magnesium_to_human.htm, viewed September 2012.

• Marni Sumbal, P.R.N., C.D. "Proper Hydration for Summer Training," Active.com, www.active.com/triathlon/Articles/Proper-Hydration-for-Summer-Training.htm, viewed September 2012.

• University of Maryland Medical Center. "Overview of Magnesium," www.umm.edu/altmed/articles/magnesium-000313.htm, created June 17, 2011.

• WebMD. "Magnesium Overview," www.webmd.com/vitamins-supplements/ingredientmono-998-MAGNESIUM.aspx?activeIngredientId=998&activeIngredientName=MAGNESIUM, created September 2012.

• WebMD. "Milk for Your Bones? Is Milk Best?" www.webmd.com/food-recipes/features/milk-for-your-bones, created October 6, 2000.

• Larry West, on water contaminates in America. "Tap Water in 42 States Contaminated by Chemicals," About.com, environment.about.com/od/waterpollution/a/tap_water_probe.htm, viewed September 14, 2012.

OTHER RECOMMENDED SOURCES

CHAPTER 1

• "Anti-Inflammatory Diet: How to Balance Omega-3 and Omega-6 Fatty Acids," The Conscious Life, theconsciouslife.com/anti-inflammatory-diet-how-to-balance-omega-3-omega-6-fats.htm, created May 23, 2012.

• Sarah Billian. "Definition of Bioavailable Vitamins," Livestrong, www.livestrong.com/article/375429-definition-of-bioavailable-vitamins, created February 7, 2011.

• "Comparison of Vitamin Levels in Raw vs. Cooked Food," Beyond Vegetarianism, www.beyondveg.com/tu-j-l/raw-cooked/raw-cooked-2f.shtml, viewed July 2012.

• Sproutnet, health benefits of and how to sprout seeds, grains, and legumes. "Sprouts for Super Nutrition," www.sproutnet.com/sprouts.htm, viewed June 2012.

• Sushma Subramanian. "Fact or Fiction: Raw Veggies Are Healthier Than Cooked Ones," Scientific American, www.scientificamerican.com/article.cfm?id=raw-veggies-are-healthier, created March 31, 2009.

• WHFoods.com. "What Can Foods Rich in Beta-Carotene Do For You?" www.whfoods.com/genpage.php?tname=nutrient&dbid=125, viewed July 11, 2012.

CHAPTER 2

• Alison and Jonathan Andrews, movie review. "The Rave Diet—Review of the Documentary 'Eating,'" Loving It Raw, www.loving-it-raw.com/rave-diet.html, viewed June 2012.

• The Engine 2 Team, on processed soy versus whole soy. "The Engine 2 Diet—What About Soy?" Engine 2 Diet, www.engine2diet.com/about_e2/FAQ, created April 11, 2012.

CHAPTER 4

• Marlene Alphonse, on food additives. "Propylene Glycol Dangers," Buzzle, www.buzzle.com/articles/propylene-glycol-dangers.html, created October 4, 2011.

• Celiac.com. "What Is Celiac Disease?" www.celiac.com, created September 25, 2012.

• Genetically Modified Foods—The Silent Killer, a Wordpress site. "Soy—The Untold Story," todayyesterdayandtomorrow.wordpress.com/2007/09/16/soy-the-untold-story, created September 16, 2007.

• Georgia Department of Agriculture. "Americans with Tree Nut Allergy," agr.georgia.gov/consumer-qs-march-2012.aspx, created March 2012.

• Sage Kalmus, C.H.H.C., "What Is Bad about Mono- and Diglycerides?" Livestrong, www.livestrong.com/article/445850-what-is-bad-about-mono-diglycerides, created May 19, 2011.

• PreventDisease.com. "Acid and Alkaline Balance—Assessing pH," preventdisease.com/fundament/articles/acid_alkaline.shtml, viewed July 2012.

• Dana Smith. "The Cookie Monster in All of Us—Sugar Addiction," Brainstudy, brainstudy.wordpress.com/2011/10/05/the-cookie-monster-in-all-of-us-sugar-addiction, created October 5, 2011.

• Davey Wavey. "Six Foods Secretly High in Sugar," Davey Wavey Fitness, www.daveywaveyfitness.com/nutrition/6-foods-secretly-high-in-sugar, created May 25, 2011.

• S.D. Wells. "Sodium Benzoate Is a Preservative That Promotes Cancer and Kills Healthy Cells," Natural News, www.naturalnews.com/033726_sodium_benzoate_cancer.html, created September 29, 2011.

CHAPTER 5

• Livestrong. "Information on Protein Foods Containing Sulfur," www.livestrong.com/article/295853-information-on-protein-foods-containing-sulfur, created June 14, 2011.

CHAPTER 6

• Food Intolerance Info. "What Are the Ten Most Common Symptoms of a Gluten Intolerance?" foodintoleranceinfo.com/gluten-intolerance/what-are-the-10-most-common-symptoms-of-a-gluten-intolerance, viewed July 2012.

CHAPTER 7

• AlgaeCal. "Magnesium-Rich Foods," www.algaecal.com/magnesium/magnesium-rich-foods.html, viewed September 2012.

• Michael Edwards. "Bottled Water vs. Tap Water," Organic Lifestyle Magazine, www.organiclifestylemagazine.com/green/issue-3/bottled-water-vs-tap-water.php, created April 2012.

• Howard Perlman. "The Water within You," USGS Water Science School, ga.water.usgs.gov/edu/propertyyou.html, viewed September 13, 2012.

• SymptomsOfDehydration.com. "Signs and Symptoms of Dehydration," www.symptomsofdehydration.com, viewed September 2012.

• Vaughn's Summaries. "High Magnesium Foods Table," www.vaughns-1-pagers.com/food/magnesium-foods.htm, viewed September 2012.

• Water Cure. "FAQ on Water," www.watercure.com/faq.html, created 2008.

ABOUT THE AUTHOR

Tina Leigh is the founder of Haute Health, a company devoted to supporting whole body transformation through therapeutic nutrition counseling and customized holistic health services. She is a natural foods chef, nutrition consultant, and certified holistic health counselor. She was the recipe developer for *The Complete Idiot's Guide to Low-Fat Vegan Cooking*, and has been featured on Fox News, The Food Network, and in *Cooking Light*.

A lover of fresh foods and all things natural since childhood, the Portland, Oregon, native pursued a career as a chef at age twenty-one. Rather than going to work in a restaurant, she chose the path of private health chef where she could use her intuitive gifts and nutrition education to nurture her clientele with therapeutic foods.

After attending college in southern Utah, where she studied business management and nutrition, she launched a meal delivery service, Urban Cuisine, in Salt Lake City, and later moved her operation to Southern California. Though her business was booming, she struggled to stay active and focused as mysterious illnesses, plaguing her since youth, kept showing up. For years, Tina had looked to conventional doctors for treatment of a long list of medical conditions. They would address symptoms with medication and send her away, only to have her soon visit again with another ailment.

After working with more than twenty doctors over the course of twenty-two years, and amassing a nearly six-figure debt, she was determined to take her health into her own hands and discover what was keeping her from living a vibrant life. She attended seminars and conferences and read every book and case study she could get her hands on about barriers to health such as chemical, radioactive, and environmental toxins, body acidity, antibiotics and hormones, food additives and preservatives, stress, and unresolved emotional pain.

Extensive research combined with experimentation led her to self-heal through eating a whole foods plant-based diet, routinely practicing yoga and meditation, by incorporating herbal medicine, and learning to heal emotional wounds, which she discovered had manifested into many of her physical illnesses. After an intense four-year recovery, she was free of almost every condition. Her wellness transformation was so powerful she was inspired to help others in their journey to health and wholeness; she attended the Institute for Integrative Nutrition to receive certification as a holistic health counselor.

Today, she works with restaurateurs to enhance their menus with fresh juices, and gluten-free and vegan cuisine, consults wellness organizations on how to develop services that will best nurture and transform the health of their clients, and shares inspirational messages of health and whole-being transformation through e-newsletters and her blog at www.hautehealthnow.com.

INDEX